Understanding
The Boat from the
Time of Jesus

Galilean Seafaring

SHELLEY WACHSMANN

cartaJerusalem

First published in 2015 by
CARTA Jerusalem

Copyright © 2015
Carta Jerusalem, Ltd.
11 Rivka Street, P.O.B. 2500,
Jerusalem 9102401, Israel
E-mail: carta@carta.co.il
www.carta-jerusalem.com

Editor: Barbara Ball
Cartography: Carta Jerusalem

References used in this book:
Gospel quotations are from the New Revised Standard Version (NRSV).

Quotes from Josephus are taken from the following translations:
The Jewish War: G. Cornfeld, B. Mazar, P. L. Maier and Josephus Flavius. 1982. *Josephus, the Jewish War: Newly Translated with Extensive Commentary and Archaeological Background Illustrations*. Grand Rapids, Michigan, Zondervan Publishing House.

Life of Josephus: 1926. *Josephus* I: *The Life and Against Apion*. Transl. H. St. J. Thackeray. (Loeb Classical Library.) London & New York. William Heinemann & G. P. Putnam's Sons.

ISBN: 978-965-220-872-9

Printed in Israel

FOREWORD

On the following pages Shelley Wachsmann weaves a marvelous tapestry of legend, Scripture and archaeology, which is held together by his extensive knowledge of seafaring life on the Kinneret Lake. No one is more qualified to guide us through the events surrounding the excavation and preservation of the first-century Galilee boat found mired in the silted lake bottom near Kibbutz Ginosar in 1986. Wachsmann was at the time Inspector of Underwater Antiquities for the Israel Department of Antiquities and Museums (the predecessor of the Israel Antiquities Authority), and he was the one tasked to investigate the new find. He provides fresh details about the race against time and the elements to rescue the boat before it was overtaken by the rising waters of the lake.

In the lead-up to this detailed account, Wachsmann navigates with aplomb through the many stories and legends told in the ancient world that make mention of the lake. While readers may be familiar with stories from the Hebrew Bible and the Gospels, the author casts his net wider and reminds us that the lake played a role in legends reaching back to the second millennium B.C. He retells a story inscribed by the Ugaritic scribe Ilimilku about prince Aqhat and the goddess Anat that ends tragically at Beit Yerah on the southwestern shores of the Sea of Galilee. This and other stories remind us of the important place the lake held in the imagination of those who lived near its shores.

Wachsmann notes that the lake has been known by many names, usually in association with a city (Kinnerot, Tiberias, Taricheae) or geographical feature (the Plain of Gennesar[eth]) that touched the lake's edge. In the first century of the Common Era we hear for the first time its Christian name—Sea of Galilee. Outside of the Gospels of Matthew, Mark and John this name never appears in any Greek, Latin, Hebrew or Aramaic literature until the Byzantine period. I have suggested elsewhere that the Christian name 'Sea of Galilee' was a type of midrashic literary creation intended to allude to Isaiah 9:1 [Hebrew 8:23]. This is the only verse in the Hebrew Bible where we find together 'sea' and 'Galilee.' Christian readers were invited to believe that not only was the activity of Jesus in the region a fulfillment of these verses, but that his very location—near the sea, by the sea or on the sea—was a fulfillment of Isaiah's words. Whatever name the local inhabitants or visitors chose to identify this relatively small body of water, its legend has traveled well beyond its rocky shores.

Between Josephus and the New Testament Gospels, we have numerous details about Jewish life and fishing on the lake in the first century. Wachsmann keeps these reports in the reader's mind as he dovetails them with his account of the discovery of the Galilee boat. He demonstrates the importance of the find for a better understanding of its first-century setting. For example, the author brings the historical descriptions together with the mosaic of a first-century boat found at nearby Magdala (Migdal) to discuss the crew size for a boat like the Galilee boat. The Magdala mosaic presents four oarsmen and a helmsman for a crew of five. This is likewise the picture we receive from Josephus' accounts.

Wachsmann reminds us that nowhere in the Gospels does it actually describe that Jesus was joined by all twelve disciples at one time in a boat. While there was capacity for them all to be included, the New Testament stories only state that he was accompanied by "his disciples" without numbering how many (e.g., Matthew 8:23; 14:22; Mark 6:45; 8:10; Luke 8:22; John 6:22). In the post-resurrection account of John 21:2–3, Simon Peter announces that he is preparing to go out on the lake to fish, and he is joined by Thomas, Nathana-el, James, John and "two other" unnamed disciples for a total of seven—apparently a five-man crew and two others to man the fishing nets. This is what we would expect, now that we are familiar with the size of the boats that sailed the lake at this time. The author's use of archaeology to illustrate and illumine our reading of the ancient reports is archaeology at its best, and it is on clear display in Wachmann's book.

Although modest in length, the reader will find within the covers of Wachmann's work a treasure trove of information, ancient and new, which is sure to prompt a healthy rethinking of old assumptions concerning seafaring on the Sea of Galilee in the distant past. We owe Wachsmann a debt of gratitude both for his efforts in the field of archaeology and for bringing the results to us in such a vivid, well-written and accessible account.

R. Steven Notley, Ph.D.
Nyack College, New York City

CONTENTS

For Mendel Nun
1918–2010

&

William 'Bill' H. Charlton, Jr.
1941–2014

The Sea of Galilee at sunset. (Photo: entb Pikiwiki Israel.)

INTRODUCTION

The ancient boat from the Sea of Galilee now exhibited at the Yigal Allon Museum at Kibbutz Ginosar speaks of pivotal times on the lake two millennia ago, when an itinerant rabbi walked its shores and sailed its waters with his followers, and changed the world forever.

This volume aims to give the non-expert reader an in-depth understanding of the boat, the story of her discovery and excavation and, most importantly, her significance for illuminating Jesus' ministry by helping us better understand its contemporaneous milieu of seafaring and fishing on the Sea of Galilee.

GALILEAN SEAFARING IN THE GOSPELS

Mark Twain, 1874

One of the most astonishing things that have yet fallen under our observation is the exceedingly small portion of the earth from which sprang the now flourishing plant of Christianity…. Leaving out two or three short journeys of the Saviour, he spent his life, preached his Gospel, and performed his miracles within a compass no longer than an ordinary county in the United States. It is as much as I can do to comprehend this stupefying fact. How it wears a man out to have to read up a hundred pages of history every two or three miles…

Mark Twain, *The Innocents Abroad*: 502

Most people visiting the Sea of Galilee for the first time are surprised by how small it is, particularly in consideration of the momentous events that took place on and around its shores. When it is full, the lake is only 21 kilometers (13 miles) long bearing north-south, and 12 kilometers (7.5 miles) wide, bearing east-west. Thousands of years ago, a large body of water known as the Lisan Lake filled the entire Jordan Valley. When the Lisan Lake retreated, it left in place the Jordan River System, with the Sea of Galilee as the central element, lying between the Hula Swamp in the north and the Dead Sea in the south.

The Sea of Galilee is not a sea: it is a freshwater inland lake. In both biblical and Talmudic sources the lake is termed *yam*, which is Hebrew for 'sea.' This same term is used to describe both large and small bodies of water, and this is why it is rendered as 'sea' in its numerous translations.

Kinneret, or *Yam* (Sea of) *Kinneret*, is the ancient Hebrew name for the Sea of Galilee. The source of this name remains elusive. One theory derives it from *kinor*, the Hebrew word for a lyre, a string instrument, which the contours of the lake roughly parallel when seen from a bird's eye view. A second tradition derives the name from *kinnara*, a sweet fruit produced in the vicinity by the Christ-thorn tree (*Ziziphus spina-christi*).

The most likely explanation for the lake's numerous names, however, is that they derive from significant cities or regions on its shores. Kinneret is the earliest name and comes from *Kinnarot*, a city located on the lake's northwestern shore. The site, now known as Tel Kinnarot (that is, the mound of Kinnarot), thrived during the Early Bronze Age (roughly four to five thousand years ago) and then again during the Late Bronze and Iron Ages. Kinnarot eventually fell, apparently to the invading Assyrian king Tiglath-pileser III, in 732 B.C.

The lake then took its name from *Biq'at Ginosar* (the Valley of Ginosar), which encompasses the northwest region adjacent to the lake, stretching from the ancient site of Migdal in the south to Kinnarot in the north. It is along this shore, not far from Migdal, where the ancient boat had slept her long sleep until her discovery in 1986.

Biq'at Ginosar is exceptionally fertile as Josephus Flavius, the first-century A.D. Jewish historian, writes:

Josephus Flavius. (From The Works of Flavius Josephus, *trans. William Whiston, 1854.)*

Thanks to the rich soil, there is not a plant that does not flourish there, and the cultivators in fact grow every species; the air is so temperate that it suits the most diverse varieties. The walnut tree, which is the most winter-loving, grows luxuriantly beside the palm tree, which thrives on heat, and side by side with the fig and olive, which require a milder air. One might deem it nature's crowning ambition to force together in a single spot, the most discordant species, and that, by a healthy rivalry, each of the seasons, as it were, wishes to claim the region for her own.

The Jewish War III:516–518

The Gospels know the lake as the *Sea of Gennesaret*, after the Valley of Ginosar. Most commonly, though, the Gospels refer to the lake as the *Sea of Galilee*, after the geographical area in which it is situated.

Herod Antipas founded the city of Tiberias in A.D. 20, in honor of the Roman emperor Tiberius. This city is unique in being the largest one ever built along the shores of the lake and also the only one that weathered the vicissitudes of history. This is why the Gospels also know the lake as the *Sea of Tiberias*.

We do not have a single written source from Jesus himself. Our knowledge of his actions and his words come down to us primarily from the New Testament Gospels. The word *gospel* comes from the Old English word *godspel*, meaning 'good tale' or 'good tidings.'

Tiglath-pileser III; relief from the king's palace at Calah, now in The British Museum. (Photo: Jastrow, via Wikimedia Commons.)

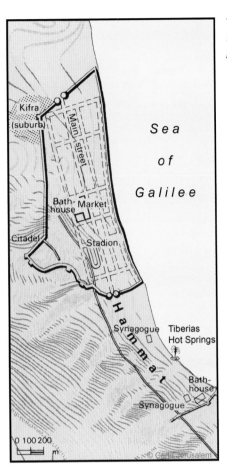

Tiberias—plan of the city in the Roman-Byzantine period.

Coin of Herod Antipas, founder of Tiberias.
(Carta Collection)

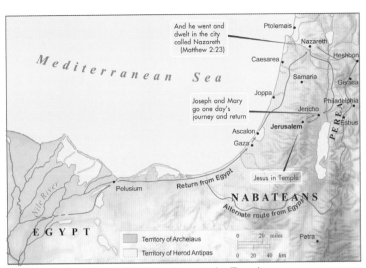

The Return from Egypt; The Boy Jesus in the Temple.

Following the death of Jesus there existed many compilations of stories, which were kept by the early Judeo-Christian believers. Numerous gospels circulated in antiquity recording the life, works and sayings of Jesus. The emergent church, however, considered most of these gospels heretical and actively suppressed them, canonizing only four of the many competing gospels—those of Matthew, Mark, Luke and John. The first three of these are referred to collectively as the Synoptic Gospels, because they follow a more-or-less similar narrative. The Gospel of John diverges significantly from the other three.

The Gospels cannot be considered biographical in the modern sense of the term: they lack any reference to entire periods in the life of Jesus. One can imagine the life of Jesus as a play in five acts, of which two are unaccounted for. We have Act I, which deals with his birth, as well as the flight to, and the return from, Egypt. Act II, which encompasses the years of Jesus' early childhood is entirely missing. In Act III Jesus appears as a 12-year-old youth accompanying his parents on a Passover visit to the Holy Temple in Jerusalem. Act IV would have covered his teenage years and his young adulthood until the start of his ministry: this, too, is missing in the Gospels.

Act V recounts the entire period of Jesus' ministry. It is primarily this part of his life in which the Gospels set out the message of Jesus. With but few exceptions, this period of his life took place on and around the Sea of Galilee, embedded in a milieu of fishermen, boats and seafaring on the lake. Despite the consideration that this period of Jesus' life is the primary focus of the Gospels, it also is telescoped into relatively few episodes.

When he began his ministry, Jesus came to the shores of the Sea of Galilee from his home and family in Nazareth. His ministry was mainly addressed to the local simple Jewish folk, 'the people of the land' (Hebrew: *am ha'aretz*) who inhabited the Jewish settlements that ringed the Sea of Galilee, particularly Capernaum, located on the northwest shore of the lake, as well as at nearby Chorazin and

Silver star in the Grotto of the Nativity, marking the traditional birthplace of Jesus in Bethlehem. (Photo: Mike Horton.)

Remains of the synagogue at Capernaum. (Photo: Britchi Mirela, via Wikimedia Commons.)

Arab fishermen using seine nets on the Sea of Galilee. (Photo: A. Oppenheimer.)

Bethsaida. Thus, while Jesus' message is universal, the setting in which it was delivered is a decidedly local one: the Sea of Galilee animated by seafaring and fishing on the lake.

The Sea of Galilee, though not large, had significant economic value. The lake teemed with fish, supplying important protein, and was, therefore, an important source of food both tasty and nutritious. Additionally, boats facilitated movement around the lakeshore.

In living memory the lake's fishermen still employed the same fishing techniques used in the time of Jesus. Only relatively recently, with the introduction of modern methods and materials, have these fishing traditions changed. In the 1960s nylon replaced cotton thread in fishing nets, making them invisible to fish. This allowed fishermen to use nocturnal fishing methods during daylight hours. Additionally, the populations of some types of indigenous fish have declined, while new species of fish have been introduced into the lake.

Four of the lake's species of edible fish. (Courtesy Helga Dudman.)

As he walked by the Sea of Galilee, he saw two brothers, Simon, who is called Peter, and Andrew his brother, casting a net into the sea—for they were fishermen.… As he went from there, he saw two other brothers, James son of Zebedee and his brother John, in the boat with their father mending their nets, and he called them.

Matthew 4:18, 21

Jesus transformed the first Apostles from being fishermen to being 'fishers of men.' Deriving his stories directly from their daily life experiences, Jesus suited his parables to their modest lifestyle so that they resonated with his followers, making it possible for them to understand and internalize the deeper meaning of his intended message. We should not be surprised, then, given the vocational background of his closest Apostles, that boats and seafaring on the Sea of Galilee figure prominently in the Gospel stories of Jesus' ministry.

The Gospels contain many references to boats. In some cases they are used for fishing while in others boats are employed for the transport of passengers around the lake. Indeed, some of the most cherished Gospel stories are those that express beliefs and numinous experiences in relation to boat-related activities. The Gospels also relate rarer uses for boats, such as being used as a podium from which Jesus speaks to masses on shore (Matthew 13:1–3; Mark 3:9, 4:1). Somewhat of the nautical 'flavor' of the Gospels comes to light in the following examples…

Again, the kingdom of heaven is like a net that was thrown into the sea and caught fish of every kind.… Matthew 13:47

Jesus' listeners were well familiar with the seine net to which Jesus compares heaven in this parable. Some of them may have just come back from fishing with a seine net. Followers who lived around the lake would not have been strangers to a seascape of seine nets spread out to dry after use.

> *...when it was full, they drew it [the seine net] ashore, sat down, and put the good into baskets but threw out the bad.*
>
> Matthew 13:48

'Good' fish, 'bad' fish? To modern ears this seems a strange indictment: Jesus here appears to be passing moral judgment on the fish. His description, however, would have been perfectly understandable to his audience. To emphasize his message concerning the kingdom of heaven, where angels would separate the righteous from the evil, Jesus compares it to fishermen on the shore separating the ritually clean (kosher) fish caught in the net, which Jews were permitted to eat (because they had both fins and scales) to the local catfish, which because it lacked scales was not considered kosher and, therefore, having no economic value, would have been cast back into the lake.

> *...go to the sea and cast a hook; take the first fish that comes up; and when you open its mouth you will find a coin....*
>
> Matthew 17:27

During the period of the Second Temple in Jerusalem, every adult Jewish male 20 years or older had to pay an annual temple tax of a half-shekel, or *didrachma*. The tax was collected in the Jewish month of *Adar*, which falls roughly equivalent to February/March: this money covered the general upkeep of the Temple and the daily burnt offerings made in the name of the people. Each community collected the taxes from its members and forwarded it to the Temple.

When the Temple tax collectors approached Simon Peter for payment, Jesus told him to go down to the Sea of Galilee and cast a hook into the lake. The first fish that Peter caught in this manner had a *stater* in its mouth, the equivalent of two *didrachmas* that covered the tax due for both of them.

Today, visitors to the Sea of Galilee can feast on a local delicacy called St. Peter's Fish, so named after Peter's famous catch. The Hebrew name for this fish, *amnun*, is a combination of two words:

St. Peter's Fish is a delicacy of the Sea of Galilee region. (Photo: Etan Tal, via Wikimedia Commons.)

Half-shekel coin, A.D. 66–70. (Photo: Classical Numismatic Group, Inc. http://www.cngcoins, via Wikimedia Commons.)

am meaning 'nurse' and *nun* meaning 'fish': the name refers to the fish's curious habit of carrying its fertilized eggs in its mouth until they hatch. *Musht*, the fish's name in Arabic, alludes to its comb-like dorsal fin. Its Latin name is *Tilapia Galilea*.

The name 'St. Peter's Fish' is so indelibly attached to this species that it may come as a surprise that this cannot possibly be the type of fish caught by St. Peter. In other words, this fish has bogus credentials.

How do we know this? Simply put, the *amnun* cannot be caught with a hook and line because it is a plankton eater. It can only be caught with a net. The fish St. Peter caught is probably to be identified with the *binit*, a member of the carp family of which there are three different species native to the Sea of Galilee. The *binit* preys on small fry and sardines and, thus, can be caught with a hook and line. When cooked the *binit* makes excellent 'gefilte fish' a traditional Jewish dish, but it does not fry well.

How, then, did the *amnun* become so indelibly connected with the Gospel story? The scope of culinary possibilities became significant beginning in the fourth century A.D., after Christianity became the Roman Empire's state religion under Constantine the Great. During the following centuries the Sea of Galilee became an important site for Christian pilgrims desiring to visit the beloved locations that they read about in the Gospels. And, where there are tourists, soon inns and restaurants will naturally spring up.

The innkeepers catering to the many Christian pilgrims arriving to the shores of the Sea of Galilee to visit its holy sites assigned the evocative name to the type of tasty fish that they could prepare most quickly for their diners. And so the *musht* acquired the traditional mantle of 'St. Peter's Fish' because it fries well.

> *One day he got into a boat with his disciples, and he said to them, "Let us go across to the other side of the lake." So they put out...*
>
> Luke 8:22

Jesus and his Disciples used boats to move about the lake. There was nothing unusual about this. Other early sources also indicate that the Sea of Galilee served as a transportation hub for passengers and commodities.

In one case Jesus, perhaps seeking relief from the crowds demanding his attention, asked to sail to the eastern side of the lake. All three Synoptic Gospels relate this event with minor variations, with the boat docking at "the land of the Gadarenes" (Matthew 8:28) or the "land of the Gerasanes" (Mark 5:1; Luke 8:26, 37).

As their boat pulled up to an uninhabited part of the coast, the group was accosted by a person possessed by a band of demons who self-identified as 'Legion.' The Gospels tell how Jesus banished the demons, allowing them instead to enter into a large herd of pigs

The Byzantine monastery at Kursi. (Photo: Shmuel Magal.)

pasturing on a nearby slope. Once possessed, the pigs promptly stampeded into the lake, drowning in its waters. Witnessing all this, the stunned herders who had been tending the pigs ran back to their city.

> *Then the whole town came out to meet Jesus; and when they saw him, they begged him to leave their neighborhood. And after getting into a boat he crossed the sea....* Matthew 8:34–9:1

The citizens soon arrived on the scene and realized that the pig herders had told the truth. There was the previously-possessed man sitting quite calmly at Jesus' feet, while their, now dead, pigs floated in the water. Instead of happiness at the demoniac's miraculous recovery, the townspeople pleaded with Jesus to leave their shores. This reaction to Jesus casting out the demons seems surprising. Why would the locals have sent Jesus away for carrying out a miracle? What did they fear?

In fact, the attitude of the locals may have been the result of economic considerations. An estimated 2,000 swine had been 'paid' in exchange for the healing of a single demented person (Matthew 5:13). The locals may have felt that at that price they could ill afford any more such cures, irrespective of how miraculous they appeared to be.

The reference to a herd of pigs is an interesting clue for determining the location where the event took place. This element positions the story on the southeastern quadrant of the Sea of Galilee, where two pagan cities flourished at that time: Hippos (Sussita) and Gadara (Hammat Gader). The other three sides of the lake abutted Jewish settlements, where pigs would have been considered unclean.

The traditional site associated with this story is Kursi, where excavations have revealed a monastery, which was built in the Byzantine period apparently to support the influx of pilgrims who wished to visit the location of the Miracle of the Swine. The monastery, built during the fifth century, continued in use for three more centuries. The site contains many beautiful mosaics depicting flora and fauna and is well worth a visit. Regrettably, in the past the heavy hand of iconoclasts destroyed many of the animals that appeared in the mosaics. Near the gates, the archaeologists discovered gaming boards consisting of rows of small shallow circles carved into the pavement slabs, created perhaps by bored guards, to pass the time while on watch.

> *When Jesus had crossed again in the boat to the other side, a great crowd gathered around him; and he was by the sea.* Mark 5:21

Upon returning from the east side of the lake, Jesus and his companions went "to his own town" of Capernaum (Matthew 9:1). Their boat must have pulled in at the settlement's harbor, as Mark (5:21) relates how a large crowd of people seeking Jesus' assistance while "he was by the sea" engulfed him immediately.

Over a dozen small fishermen's harbors of varying shapes and sizes ringed the Sea of Galilee during the time of Jesus. The builders had considered the directions of treacherous local winds and the prevalent waves specific to each site and had built the structures accordingly. The financial means—*or lack thereof*—of the settlements adjacent to the harbors also played a role in determining their construction. Most harbors consisted of some form of a stone breakwater protecting an enclosed basin, while an adjacent promenade facilitated access to the protected area.

Capernaum's harbor has a unique, and frankly strange, design, which may have resulted from its extended period of use. The city had a long history of habitation, from the second century B.C. to the tenth century A.D. and, thus, the harbor may have been built in phases during that time. This complex had a promenade that extended over 800 meters (2,625 feet), with piers jutting out into the lake to protect boats from the south wind. Three of the piers are triangular-shaped, pointing into the lake from the promenade.

Apparently, during the time of Jesus' ministry, a customs office was located somewhere along this coast. Here new arrivals had to pay taxes to Herod Antipas. The Jewish inhabitants of Capernaum reviled the officials who collected these taxes, seeing the men as collaborators in an excessively harsh and corrupt political system. One of the Apostles may have been such a tax collector before joining Jesus' entourage (Matthew 9:9, 10:3).

> *When it is evening, you say, "It will be fair weather, for the sky is red." And in the morning, "It will be stormy today, for the sky is red and threatening." You know how to interpret the appearance of the sky, but you cannot interpret the signs of the times.* Matthew 16:2–3

Mosaic pavement in the basilica at Kursi. (Photo: Shmuel Magal.)

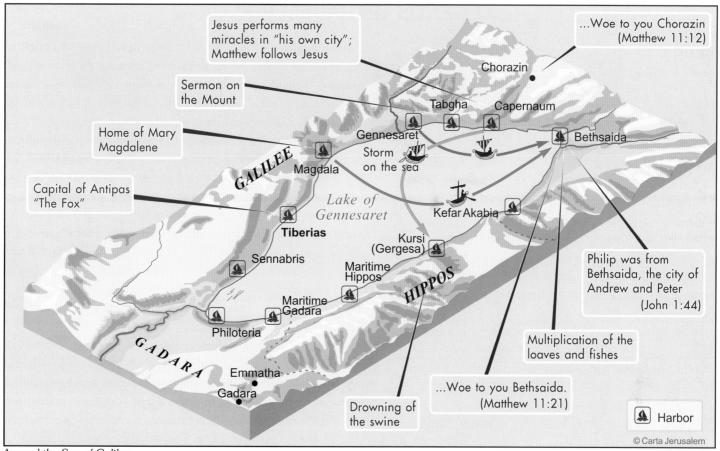

Around the Sea of Galilee.

We witness another subtle indication of Jesus' familiarity with the nautical life in his knowledge of seafaring weather lore. Jesus warns of a storm in his forecast, which is feared by the sailor, but not necessarily by the farmer. We know this saying today in the following rhyme:

> Red sky in the morning,
> Sailors take warning.
> Red sky at night,
> Sailors delight.

This saying has meteorological merit. The weather flow is generally westerly in the northern horse latitudes, so a red sunset indicates that the incoming weather is dust-laden and, thus, dry.

> And leaving the crowd behind, they took him with them in the boat, just as he was. Other boats were with him. A great windstorm arose, and the waves beat into the boat, so that the boat was already being swamped.
> Mark 4:36–37

The lake can be fickle, with the possibility of sudden and dangerous storms. Here we see a noticeable difference between ancient seafaring on the Mediterranean and on the Sea of Galilee. Mediterranean seafaring was a distinctly seasonal occupation, mainly relegated to the period from spring to fall, when seafarers could expect clear skies and storms were fewer. Of course, some ships did sail in the winter months, but in antiquity sailing was severely curtailed during the off-season. St. Paul acknowledges this phenomenon when he pointed out to the centurion who was taking him to Rome for trial that it was late in the sailing season and that the grain ship on which the two men had taken passage should remain in the Cretan port of Fair Haven rather than heading for the port of Phoenix:

> We sailed slowly for a number of days and arrived with difficulty off Cnidus, and as the wind was against us, we sailed under the lee of Crete off Salmone. Sailing past it with difficulty, we came to a place called Fair Havens, near the city of Lasea.
>
> Since much time had been lost and sailing was now dangerous, because even the Fast had already gone by, Paul advised them, saying, "Sirs, I can see that the voyage will be with danger and much heavy loss, not only of the cargo and the ship, but also of our lives."
> Acts 27:7–10

St. Paul's pleas went unheeded. The ship carrying him sailed directly into a storm, ultimately to be shipwrecked off Malta (Acts 27:11–44). As opposed to this seasonality of Mediterranean seafaring, due to the relatively short distances involved, boats on the Sea of Galilee sailed throughout the winter months as well.

There is a daily order to the winds around the Sea of Galilee during the summer and fall, but in the winter months the weather system can be chaotic, and the winds have a tendency to shift, blowing from one direction and then another. It is also during the winter months that a strong east wind, known in the region as the *Sharkia* or *Hamsin*, comes howling down the Golan Heights on the east side of the lake and stirs up the lake's waters, raising waves that batter its western shores. *Sharkias* come at a frequency of about once every fortnight and generally last for a few days.

There is, of course, one last strand that connects Jesus to the wooden-planked boats on the Sea of Galilee: Jesus was a carpenter by trade, as was Joseph before him:

> Is not this the carpenter…? Is not this the carpenter's son?
> Mark 6:3; Matthew 13:55

LEGENDS & TRAVELERS

Legends

I have a word to tell you,
a story to recount to you:
the word of the tree and the charm of the stone,
the whisper of the heavens to the earth,
of the seas to the stars…
Come and I will reveal it.

From *The Baal Cycle*
as transcribed by Ilimilku (Coogan 1978: 92)

Yam Kinneret, Sea of Gennesaret, Sea of Tiberias, Sea of Galilee: this multi-named lake inspired many legends and fables which are endurably linked to its waters. Throughout time people have given to the lake both mystical and mythical qualities, making it truly a 'sea of legends.' These stories impart to the Sea of Galilee a peculiar ambience that speaks of bygone days and is as much a part of her as the fish that swim in her waters.

The cast of characters in these legends is indeed a marvelous one. They include a jealous goddess, a satanic bird, a lascivious river and a wandering well with magical properties. And let's not forget a legion of deaf she-demons….

The jealous goddess.—The earliest written reference we have to the Sea of Galilee was inscribed long ago, and remarkably far away from its shores. It seems somehow fitting that this legendary lake first appears in, well, in a legend.

Over three thousand years ago Ilimilku, a young (at the time) student scribe, held a moist clay tablet in his hand and began to transcribe on it a legend as told to him by his master, Attanu-Purlianni.

Attanu-Purlianni served then as the high priest to the Canaanite god Baal. As the high priest began to tell the story, Ilimilku wrote it down, filling up first one side of the tablet and then the other. When he ran out of room on that first tablet, he continued on a second, and then a third one.

Ilimilku's tablets remained safely tucked away in the house of the high priest until a century and a half later, around 1185 B.C., when barbarians invading from the sea destroyed the city. The city disappeared into dust, entirely forgotten through the ages.

A bronze figurine, possibly representing Baal, with right arm raised. 14th–12th centuries B.C., found at Ras Shamra (ancient Ugarit). (Now in the Louvre Museum, Paris. Photo: Jastrow, via Wikimedia Commons.)

In antiquity, Ugarit, for that was the city's name, had been a major port of trade. It lay approximately due east of Cyprus in what is today Syria. Ugarit only came to light in 1928, when a farmer accidentally struck a rock-built tomb while plowing a field at Ras Shamra (Arabic for 'Cape Fennel'), the site's modern name.

Since that day, the archaeologist's spade has revealed impressive remains at Ugarit, including many inscribed clay tablets. Ugarit had been a remarkably literate city. The tablets were written mainly, although not exclusively, in two cuneiform scripts: Akkadian, which served as the *lingua franca* of the time, and Ugaritic, an early alphabetic script consisting of a limited number of cuneiform characters used to transcribe the West Semitic language that was commonly spoken in the city. Among the most important documents discovered are those of Ilimilku: these tablets detail the mythological foundations of the Syro-Canaanite religion as practiced in Ugarit during the Late Bronze Age.

The story that Ilimilku wrote down that day related a legend that was already ancient in his own day. The tale begins with a wise and righteous king named Danel, who lacked a male heir. To remedy this situation he offered up sacrifices to the gods of Canaan for seven days. Responding to these heartfelt pleas for help, Baal approached El, the elderly head god of the Canaanite pantheon. El agreed to Baal's request and returned to Danel his missing 'passion.' Soon his wife was pregnant.

They named the child Aqhat, and the youth's pride and joy was a remarkable composite bow, created especially for him by the Canaanite god of inventions, *Kothar-wa-Khasis*, their equivalent to the Greek god Hephaestus. Unfortunately for Aqhat, however, this bow caught the attention of the goddess Anat.

Anat offered him gold and silver for the bow, but Aqhat politely declined Anat's offer. In place of the bow, Aqhat offered to bring Anat the finest-quality materials required to build a composite bow like his: these included wood, tendons and the horns of wild goats.

Anat remained adamant in her desire for Aqhat's bow. She now promised him immortality in return for his bow. Again Aqhat refused to do the goddess's bidding. Rash in his youth, Aqhat called Anat a liar, stating that she would not be able to make good on an offer such as this. Even the gods could not change the fact that humans were subject to mortality. Additionally, in what would be considered today a highly sexist comment, Aqhat claimed that bows were for men and not for women.

Big mistake. Anat, while female, was hardly a shrinking violet. She reigned as the goddess of love and war, a somewhat interesting combination of responsibilities. She is described as wearing a grisly necklace decorated with the heads of men killed in battle. And from her belt—apparently designed by the same couturier—the severed hands of men dangled in place of tassels. Clearly, Anat was not a lady to be taken lightly.

Exasperated by Aqhat's refusal to hand over his bow, Anat decided to kill Aqhat and, thus, to secure his bow. Anat enlisted Yatpan, an assassin whom she placed in her pouch as she soared with the birds of prey high above the unsuspecting Aqhat.

Cuneiform tablet of the legend of Danel and his son Aqhat, from Ugarit, c. 14th–13th centuries B.C. *(Now in the Louvre Museum, Paris. Fouilles C. Schaeffer, 1931, via Wikimedia Commons)*

Aqhat had been dining in the city of Abiluma when Anat swooped down and Yatpan struck. Aqhat died a needless death. Although Ilimalku's text is partially broken here, it is clear that Aqhat's bow, the acquisition of which was the reason for his murder, was somehow damaged, and apparently lost, when it fell into a nearby body of water.

Aqhat's death caused the cessation of fertility. Crops began to whither in the fields. When Danel learned of his son's fate he mourned his loss. To retrieve Aqhat's remains for burial he asked Baal to shatter the vultures' wings, to allow him to search for the mangled remains in their gizzards. After decimating the local vulture population, Danel discovered Aqhat's fat and bones in Samal, "mother of all vultures." The grieving Danel then buried Aqhat's remains.

Danel laid a curse on three places that had been guilty of witnessing Aqhat's murder: a "pool of water"; Abiluma, the site of the crime; and a third site with an unusually long name—*Mararat tagullal-banir*.

Danel mourned Aqhat for seven years. Considering Aqhat's previous male chauvinist comments to Anat, it is perhaps ironic that it was his sister, Pagat, who set out on a mission of revenge, determined to kill Yatpan in retribution for the murder of her brother.

In preparation for this, Pagat went down to the sea to bathe, put on makeup and dress in the clothing of a hero. She armed herself with dagger and sword and then, over all this, she put on women's clothing.

It was a day's hike from where she had bathed in the sea to Yatpan's encampment. Upon arriving there, Pagat plied him with wine as he foolishly related to her how he had killed Aqhat.

Unfortunately, this is where Ilimilku's third and last tablet breaks off. We can imagine Yatpan in his cups and Pagat, no doubt with a deadly glint in her eye, waiting for the right moment to strike.

Ugaritic scholars have long debated the location of the Aqhat epic. Some scholars have plausibly situated the action in and around the Sea of Galilee. If so, then this is the earliest recorded reference to the Sea of Galilee (Yam Kinneret).

Several clues support this interpretation. First, the site where Danel buries Aqhat's remains, *bmdgt bknrt*, can be translated "in the fishing-grounds of [the Sea of] Kinneret." The second clue that Ilimilku has given us relates to Abiluma, the site of Aqhat's murder. Ilimilku explains that this is the "city of Prince Moon" (Ugaritic: *ablm qrt zbl yrh*). If the action is indeed taking place near the Sea of Galilee, then only one location can claim this title: Tel Beit Yerah, a large settlement on the southwestern shore of the lake, near where the Jordan River begins its course to the Dead Sea. Beit Yerah, a name that survived down to the Roman-Byzantine period, means "House (or temple) of the Moon(-god)."

The idea of burial in the Sea of Galilee seems strange to our modern sensibilities, but a more recent medieval Arabic legend identifies the same lake as the final resting place of King Solomon, one of Judaism's most illustrious leaders.

Tel Beit Yerah ("The Mound of the House [that is, Temple] of the Moon [-god]"), on the southwestern shore of the Sea of Galilee. (Photo: Hanay, via Wikimedia Commons)

The satanic bird.—According to one Jewish legend, the Sea of Galilee existed, floating alone in space before the Lord created the earth. And on its waters swam a large bird named Satanel.

"Who are you?" the Lord asked the bird.

"I am God," replied the pompous bird.

"But then, if you are God, who am I?" asked the Lord.

"You? Why you are God of all the gods and Lord of the Universe!" said the bird.

Then the Lord commanded Satanel to dive down into the lake and retrieve from it earth and flint. The Lord used the earth to create the land and by striking the flint he brought forth the angels.

Satanel absorbed all these wonders and wanted to duplicate the Lord's mighty deeds: God, however, became displeased with the bird's ambition and removed the letters *el*, which means 'god' from Satanel's name, and this is how he became Satan, the embodiment of evil.

The lascivious river.—The Jordan River winds its way down to the northern end of the Sea of Galilee from the former Hula swamp in a straightforward manner, entering the lake near the ancient site of Bethsaida-Julias, which has seen extensive excavations in

The meandering Jordan River. (Photo: W. Robert Moore. From The National Geographic Magazine, *Dec. 1938.*)

recent years. The river exits the lake next to Tel Beit Yerah at the southwestern extremity of the lake.

From Tel Beit Yerah, however, the Jordan River cuts a particularly convoluted path. The distance from the southern end of the Sea of Galilee to the northern extremity of the Dead Sea is about 104 kilometers (65 miles), but it takes the river 166 kilometers (103 miles) of serpentine meanderings to reach the Dead Sea. Legend supplies an explanation for the Jordan's tortuous path.

The Jordan River long ago did not flow through the Sea of Galilee. One evening, so the story goes, the river developed a desire for the gentle lake. Incapable of quenching his longings for the beautiful body of water, the Jordan swelled from his cave at Banias and flowed ever forward, forming a path between the mountains and through the ravines.

Upon reaching the Sea of Galilee, the waters of the Jordan mingled with those of the lake and the two became lovers. This angered the Lord, for the river had not received permission from on high to cut this new route. So, the Lord commanded that the surrounding mountains create a valley between the two lovers. Once this had been carried out, He flushed the Jordan out of the Sea of Galilee.

The Jordan, writhing in anguish, spilled out of the lake and meandered southward willy-nilly, dizzy and sorrowful. Then, as he descended into the maws of the Dead Sea, the river died as his waters turned bitter and lifeless.

The wandering well.—During the forty-year wanderings of the Israelites in Sinai, water was a scarce commodity. After the rebellious multitude accused Moses of bringing them to their death, the Lord ordered Moses to strike the stone at Horeb, from which water then flowed (Exodus 17:6). Later, the Israelites came to a site named *Beer*, which means 'well' in Hebrew (Numbers 21:16). "That is the well of which the Lord said to Moses, 'Gather the people together and I will give them water,'" the Bible relates.

Tradition has it that these two biblical references refer to the same well at two different locations. This unusual 'moving' well, it is claimed, was one of the Lord's last creations prior to resting on the sixth day of Creation. The well—named after Miriam, the sister of Moses—was indeed miraculous, for it traveled with the Children of Israel. During their wanderings up from the valleys and down from the mountains, Miriam's Well was always there to refresh them. Whenever the Israelites needed water the camp leaders would gather around the well and sing its song:

> Spring up, O well!—Sing to it—
> the well that the leaders sank,
> and the nobles of the people dug,
> with the scepter, with the staff.
>
> Numbers 21:17–18

The well's waters would then bubble up and rise in a column supplying water to all the Twelve Tribes. After they crossed the Jordan River and had conquered the land of Canaan, however, each of the tribes went its own way, settling its own territory. No longer in need of Miriam's Well, the tribes left it abandoned and ignored. The miraculous well no doubt felt lonely and unappreciated

Engraving of Moses striking the stone at Horeb. (From The Bible Panorama, *or* The Holy Scriptures in picture and story *by William A. Foster, 1891.*)

after all the attention it had received during the years of wandering. Tradition relates that Miriam's Well sank into the depths of the Sea of Galilee, where it is said to remain to this day.

According to Jewish sources, the waters of Miriam's Well have the twin qualities of physical healing and spiritual awakening. Safed, a Galilean settlement perched in the mountains overlooking the Sea of Galilee, served as a center for Jewish scholars who studied the Kabbala, the philosophical treatise of Jewish mysticism. These mystics, known as Kabbalists, took the tradition of Miriam's Well seriously. Rabbi Haim Vital, a leading Kabbalist, relates how in his youth, when he had come to Safed to study under the preeminent sixteenth-century Kabbalist, Rabbi Isaac Luria, who is better known as the Ari (Lion), the older man had brought him to Tiberias. In a boat on the Sea of Galilee the Ari had his young apprentice drink from the lake's waters and, when he had done so, the Ari explained that now that he had sipped from the waters of Miriam's Well he would surely be better able to comprehend the mysteries of the Kabbala.

Richard Pococke, an early British explorer who visited the Holy Land in the mid-18th century, records a similar experience:

Richard Pococke
(Musée d'art et d'histoire de Genève. Photo: Sailko, via Wikimedia Commons.)

> *A learned Jew, with whom I discoursed at Saphet [Safed], lamented that he could not have an opportunity, when he was in Tiberias, to go in a boat to see the well of Miriam in this lake, which, he said, according to their Talmudic writers, was fixed in this sea, after it had accompanied the children of Israel through the wilderness and that the water of it might be seen continually rising up.*

Richard Pockocke, *A Description of the East*: 70

A legion of deaf she-demons.—Hammat is the original name for the hot springs south of Tiberias. The reason why these springs are eternally hot, according to another legend, is that before reaching the earth's surface they flow by the gates of Hell. Thus, in the Aramaic language the waters received the name *Moked de Teverya*, 'the Flames of Tiberias.'

In Arabic, however, the hot springs are called *Hammam Malikna Suleiman*, 'the baths of our King Solomon.' This name derives from a legend that connects the hot springs of Tiberias with a direct intervention by that wisest of men.

According to this legend a group of sick men beseeched Solomon to help them cure their afflictions. Taking pity on the men, Solomon called up a troop of demons and commanded them to go forthwith to the shores of the Sea of Galilee, to a place where a cold freshwater spring flowed into the lake.

"Go down into the bowels of the earth," Solomon ordered the demons, "and heat the spring's waters."

Obeying the king, the demons immediately raced to the spring, disappeared underground and began heating the water.

The Book of Ecclesiastes is traditionally assigned to Solomon. The book contains a verse that the New Revised Standard Version of the Bible translates as follows:

> *I also gathered for myself silver and gold and treasure of kings and the provinces; I got singers, both men and women, and delights of the flesh, and many concubines.*

Ecclesiastes 2:8

After "the delights of the flesh" in the Hebrew text come two words, *shidah v'shidot*, the meaning of which is unclear. They may be translated "she-demon and she-demons." Due to their obscurity these two words have received various translations. For example, the King James Bible renders them as "musical instruments, and that of all sorts."

Midrash Kohelet Rabbah, which is an exposition, or commentary, on Ecclesiastes, interprets this sentence so that the "delights of the flesh" refer to the hot baths of Tiberias and the "she-demon and she-demons" equate with the demonic host who heats the waters.

Solomon, in his wisdom, knew that when the demons heard of his death they would have no further compulsion to heat the waters, so to prevent them from abandoning their task of heating the waters of Tiberias he made the demons deaf.

So, if you visit the hot springs in Tiberias—today they are a popular gathering place for both Israelis and tourists—remember that the heated medicinal waters are brought to you courtesy of a band of deaf she-demons, who have been toiling away since the Iron Age keeping the waters hot and who are thankfully oblivious to the passing of Solomon millennia ago.

Early Travelers to the Sea of Galilee

After the Crusader period Europe's fascination with the Holy Land waned. Following centuries of neglect, exploitation and onerous taxation the land reverted to near wilderness. Then, beginning in the 19th century, a cadre of Westerners initiated the arduous task of reclaiming the past. These hardy explorers were a determined lot who searched for the locations and the truths behind what they had read in their history books and had studied in the Scriptures.

Few of these trailblazers, however, were more determined, or more innovative in their methods, than John MacGregor.

MacGregor in his beloved Rob Roy *at the mouth of the Jordan. (From MacGregor 1870: 287.)*

MacGregor captured by the Hula Swamp Bedouin. (From MacGregor 1870: 255.)

MacGregor paddled the largely unknown waterways of the Middle East in a custom-built kayak, which he named the *Rob Roy*, after the eighteenth-century Scottish folk hero. The *Rob Roy* was 14 feet (4.27 meters) long, 26 inches (66 centimeters) in breadth and only a foot (30 centimeters) in depth: shallow in draft and highly maneuverable, the vessel permitted its pilot to explore all but the most overgrown of waterways.

MacGregor began his trip to the Holy Land by sailing down the Suez Canal while it was still under construction in October 1868. He followed this with an exploration of the Nile Delta. At all times his eye was attuned to the beauty of nature, the impression of a sunset.

At Port Said, MacGregor embarked on a ship to Beirut and from there struck out for Lebanon and Syria: in January 1869 he arrived at the Jordan Valley. He was particularly keen to locate the sources of the Jordan River before it entered the Sea of Galilee, a task for which the *Rob Roy* was ideally suited.

When he returned home, MacGregor wrote down his adventures in a book entitled *The Rob Roy on the Jordan, Nile, Red Sea & Gennesareth, &c.* The book became a bestseller in its day and saw eight editions, making its author justly famous.

MacGregor described his tiny vessel in loving terms, praising her beauty and dexterity. For him the boat was very much alive, with a spirit, a character and personality of her own:

> …Are we quite sure that there is no feeling in the "heart of oak," no sentiment under bent birch ribs; that a canoe, in fact, has no character? Let the landsman say so, yet will not I. Like others of her sex, she has her fickle tempers. One day pleasant, and the next out of humour; led like a lamb through this rapid, but cross and pouting under sail on that rough lake. And like her sex, she may be resisted, coerced nay, convinced, but in the end, she will always have her own way.

> John MacGregor, *The Rob Roy on the Jordan, Nile, Red Sea & Gennesareth, &c.*: 113

This gentleman explorer was already middle-aged when he embarked on his Middle Eastern trip in his beloved *Rob Roy*. MacGregor was convinced that this was the ideal age for a person to travel: he felt, and perhaps rightly so, that at that time in life a person is more open to new experiences and more likely to appreciate them.

Michael Hany, with whom MacGregor rendezvoused at Ismalia, served as his dragoman: a combination guide, translator, organizer, butler and friend. This partnership was invaluable to MacGregor who repeatedly emphasizes the devotion of his brave companion.

Three small tributaries—the Banias, the Dan and the Hatzbani Rivers—form the sources of the Jordan River. Once unified, the stream winds its way first through the region of the Hula Swamp, the ancient Lake Semachonitis, before entering the Sea of Galilee.

With the creation of the State of Israel in 1948, however, most of the Hula was reclaimed, turning a malarial swamp into arable agricultural land in a project known in Hebrew as *yibush ha-bitzot* (draining the swamps). Today, only a small nature reserve survives of the original wetlands navigated by MacGregor.

Unquestionably, MacGregor's most remarkable story, as well as his most perilous adventure, transpired during his exploration of the northern regions of the Hula. In those days, the Bedouin who lived in the swamp were not particularly known for their kindness to strangers, or as MacGregor notes, they "had but a poor certificate of character from the tales of travellers." Cognizant of this danger, MacGregor sent Hany ahead, to set up camp at the southwestern edge of the swamp, while he himself, determined to explore the Jordan's course as it transversed the swamp, paddled into the morass.

The serpentine meanderings of the river as it entered the Hula required MacGregor to navigate them by 'waltzing' the *Rob Roy* through the maze, at times sailing bow first, and at others stern first. As MacGregor concentrated on his intricate maneuvers, one of the locals spotted him. In seconds the banks of the river bristled with hostile screaming Bedouin.

At first, the river's fast-flowing current sped the *Rob Roy* and her captain out of harm's way. Downriver, however, some other locals spotted the strange-looking intruder in his narrow craft and now the pursuit began in earnest. Several of the men removed their scant clothing and swam after the *Rob Roy*. Eventually, by swimming and cutting through bends in the river, the Bedouin caught up with MacGregor. Turning a sharp bend he found his way blocked by a row of his pursuers lined up across the river. Writes MacGregor:

> In such times 'tis best to wait for events and not to make them. All were silent as I quietly floated near one of the swimmers, then suddenly

MacGregor, still seated in the Rob Roy, *is carried to the Bedouin encampment. (From MacGregor 1870: frontispiece.)*

splashed him in the face with my paddle and instantly escaped through the interval with vigorous strokes.

John MacGregor, The Rob Roy on the Jordan,
Nile, Red Sea & Gennesareth, &c.: 253

But it was to no avail: in the end the Bedouin captured the *Rob Roy*. Still sitting in the vessel, MacGregor found himself lifted physically out of the water by a dozen of the locals and carried to their village. MacGregor extricated himself from his predicament only thanks to his icy nerves of steel and Hany's stalwart assistance—and, of course, to baksheesh.

The celebrated Sea of Galilee is not so large a sea as Lake Tahoe by a good deal—it is just two-thirds as large. And when we come to speak of beauty, this sea is no more to be compared to Tahoe than a meridian of longitude is to a rainbow.

Mark Twain, The Innocents Abroad: 507

For those who wanted to see the Holy Land in a somewhat more pleasant manner in the nineteenth century, pilgrim tourism was booming. The good ship *Quaker City* sailed from New York in 1867 on a pleasure-cruise-pilgrimage to Europe, the Holy Land and Egypt. And on her deck stood Samuel Longhorne Clemens, a young American writer best known by his pen name: Mark Twain.

During his trip Twain wrote reports to newspapers in San Francisco and New York. Later he used these letters to the folks back home as the basis for his book, *The Innocents Abroad*. His description of the Holy Land, written about a century and a half ago, makes for fascinating reading today, not only because of Twain's sharp wit, but also because of the vivid picture he paints for us of the land and its inhabitants at that time.

After the *Quaker City* anchored in Beirut, the pilgrims split into two groups. Twain joined the 'long trip,' which wound its way from Beirut to Baalbek, Damascus, the Sea of Galilee, the Dead Sea and Jerusalem, finally rendezvousing with the *Quaker City* in Jaffa. The group set out on horseback with Abraham, a Jew, serving as the group's dragoman.

From the start, Twain had not taken kindly to the American Christian pilgrims with whom he shared the voyage. For Twain they were over-religious and under-considerate: at the same time

Tiberias and the Sea of Galilee. (From Twain 1870: 506.)

"The fare was too high." The boat sailed away. (From Twain 1870: 497.)

gushing emotionally or lacking totally in feeling. They were, in Twain's eyes, the New Philistines, clambering to break off pieces of stone as souvenirs from each ancient site they visited.

As they neared the Sea of Galilee, Twain's companions talked excitedly of 'taking ship' and sailing on the very waters across which the boats of the Apostles had once sailed. Sighting a boat, one of only two that they saw on the lake, the pilgrims eagerly hailed it. Upon the vessel's approach they ordered Abraham to negotiate a fare.

The Galilean boatmen demanded two Napoleons, equal to eight of their American dollars. The pilgrims tried to haggle down the price. The boat sailed away into the lake, leaving the petulant pilgrims high and dry on the shore—much to their chagrin and Twain's delight.

The Holy Land of the 19th century through which Twain, MacGregor and others traveled was unlike the Land of Israel that one experiences today. As a result of centuries of disregard and mismanagement by absentee landowners, the land had been stripped bare of its natural resources and fertility. Twain took pleasure in ridiculing the tourist books of his day, which described the land in glowing terms, turning parched wastelands into verdant vistas. He obviously considered himself above such drivel. The descriptions of his experiences that Twain wrote home were of what he saw, without any glossing. He saw himself as a completely objective and rational reporter. Or at least that is what he believed.

Indeed, Twain was even disappointed with the Sea of Galilee, which in his view came in a poor second to his beloved Lake Tahoe. And yet, this hardened cynic could not entirely ignore the lure of the lake. As his companions slumbered peacefully one evening, Twain penned the following impressions on the shores of the Sea of Galilee:

Night is the time to see Galilee...when the day is done, even the unimpressible must yield to the dreamy influences of this tranquil starlight. The old traditions of the place steal upon his memory and haunt his reveries, and then his fancy clothes all sights and sounds with the supernatural. In the lapping of the waves upon the beach, he hears the dip of ghostly oars; in the secret noises of the night he hears spirit voices: in the soft sweep of the breeze, the rush of invisible wings.

Mark Twain, The Innocents Abroad: 512

THE DISCOVERY & THE EXCAVATION

The Discovery

Christian art through the ages is replete with scenes of Jesus and his Disciples sailing on the Sea of Galilee. The following three images are among the most famous: Raphael's *The Miraculous Draught of Fishes* (1515), Rembrandt's *Storm on the Sea of Galilee* (1663) and Delacroix's *Christ on the Lake of Gennesaret* (1853–1854). Study carefully the boats appearing in each of these representations. What is similar to all three of the boats?

Raphael's The Miraculous Draught of Fishes *(1515).*

Delacroix's Christ on the Lake of Gennesaret *(1853–1854).*

Rembrandt's Storm on the Sea of Galilee *(1663).*

ANSWER:

Absolutely nothing! In truth, for centuries no one knew what a Sea of Galilee boat from the time of Jesus might have looked like.

This all changed in 1986. At the time Israel was in the grip of a *severe drought*. Winter rains barely fell. The ensuing drought caused the waters of the Sea of Galilee to retreat, exposing large stretches of the lake's bottom. In January of that year two brothers, members of Kibbutz Ginosar, Yuval ('Yuvi') and Moshe ('Moshele') Lufan, decided to look for an ancient boat on the mud flats revealed by the receding waters. They surveyed an area south of the Kibbutz, near the ancient site of Migdal—home of Mary Magdalene ('Mary of Migdal') where the spinning tires of a vehicle stuck in the mud had cast up coins and other artifacts. On closer inspection the brothers found iron nails, and then the outline of the edge of a wooden plank, indicating a boat buried entirely in the mud.

Yuvi Lufan stands on the outline of the boat. (Photo: S. Wachsmann. Courtesy Yigal Allon Museum.)

Shell-first construction. (Drawing: D. Johnson. Courtesy Institute of Nautical Archaeology.)

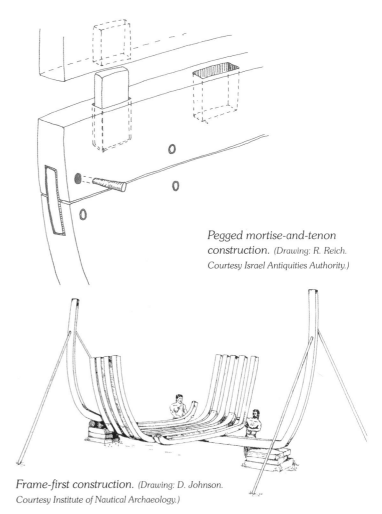

Pegged mortise-and-tenon construction. (Drawing: R. Reich. Courtesy Israel Antiquities Authority.)

Frame-first construction. (Drawing: D. Johnson. Courtesy Institute of Nautical Archaeology.)

Could the vessel be ancient? The Lufans contacted Mendel Nun of Kibbutz Ginosar, a man who had dedicated his life to the study of the Sea of Galilee and who made a significant contribution to our understanding of life on the lake in antiquity. Mendel relayed information of the discovery to the Israel Department of Antiquities and Museums (now the Israel Antiquities Authority), the governmental body responsible for Israel's archaeological heritage.

At the time I served as the Department's Inspector of Underwater Antiquities. News of the discovery, "a shipwreck—possibly ancient," reached my desk. The following day, Mendel Nun, the Lufan brothers, my colleague Kurt Raveh and I drove out to the site of the discovery.

Ancient seacraft on the Mediterranean Sea were built in what might seem today an unusual method. This form of 'shell-first' construction, in which the planks of the hull were edge joined with pegged 'mortise-and-tenon' joints does not require caulking: the water swells the wood, resulting in water-tight seams. This type of construction appears in the Mediterranean as early as the late fourteenth century B.C. and continues in use till the end of the Byzantine period. At that time the 'frame-first' skeleton-based construction that is commonly used today in building ships gradually replaced it. Mortise-and-tenon construction disappears in the Mediterranean completely by the eleventh century.

Opening a small section of that uppermost plank revealed clear evidence of pegged mortise-and-tenon joinery. We, thus, knew immediately that this was an ancient boat, although we didn't know how old yet.

In our excitement, we barely noticed that it had begun to rain. Soon torrents of water descended upon us as we all piled into my jeep. The cloudburst was short-lived, stopping as suddenly as it had started, but it left behind a magnificent double-rainbow cascading into the Sea of Galilee—as if we had ordered it from Central Casting.

Opening a small section of the uppermost plank revealed pegged mortise-and-tenon joinery. (Photo: S. Wachsmann. Courtesy Israel Antiquities Authority.)

…a double rainbow…as if ordered from Central Casting… (Photo: M. Lufan. Courtesy Israel Antiquities Authority.)

The probe excavation. *(Photo: S. Wachsmann. Courtesy Israel Antiquities Authority.)*

The cooking pot (casserole) and oil lamp found during the probe excavation. (Courtesy Israel Antiquities Authority.)

During the next two days we carried out a probe excavation in which we examined a few small sections along the boat's length to try to better understand how much of the hull survived beneath the mud and also to determine the date of the boat. This preliminary work revealed two ceramic vessels: a cooking pot, or casserole, and an oil lamp. Both artifacts date to the early Roman period (mid-first century B.C. to mid-first century A.D.), but their connection to the vessel remained illusive because the pottery had not been a part of the boat's cargo. Still, at least the finds indicated a period of human activity in the immediate vicinity of the boat.

Once we completed the probe excavation, on Friday, February 7th, 1986, we reburied the boat and took additional precautions to protect its location in order to keep the discovery a secret until the now-rising waters of the lake could cover the site. By that Sunday, however, news of the discovery had leaked to the press, who immediately christened her 'the Jesus Boat.' This journalistic canard is simply silly. Of course, no single boat can be connected with Jesus and nowhere do we read that Jesus owned a boat. He never spoke of "my boat," nor do the Gospel writers ever refer to "his boat." Apparently, Jesus made use of many boats; that is why the term 'Jesus Boat' is a particularly inappropriate name for this ancient vessel: it implies a connection for which any proof is lacking.

Almost every body of water has at least one legend telling of a lost treasure. Such is certainly the case with the Sea of Galilee. Rumors have abounded for years regarding an Ottoman ship that sank there during World War I carrying a payload of gold coins for the Turkish army. This tale now became associated with the boat: treasure hunters began searching for a 'Boat of Jesus' full of nonexistent treasure. Late that Tuesday night Yuvi and Moshele, who had been observing the site from a distance, noticed inquisitive figures with flashlights near it. They contacted me. I drove out to the site and the three of us mounted a nerve-wracking night vigil.

No additional intruders appeared, but it was now clear that the boat was in serious danger. The history of archaeology around the world is studded with cringe-worthy examples of invaluable sites and artifacts being destroyed when looters preempted the archaeologists. To protect the boat, therefore, the Department of Antiquities ordered its immediate excavation.

An excavation requires time to plan and to organize. It requires a staff, materials and equipment. Often months or even years go by between the conceptualization and the implementation of an archaeological project: but the excavation was to begin three days hence, on February 16th. I quickly assembled the excavation team.

A critical member of the team would be a ship reconstructor—someone to make sense of the hull that we would be unearthing. I contacted Professor J. Richard 'Dick' Steffy of the Institute of Nautical Archaeology (INA) at Texas A&M University. Prior to his death in 2007, Dick was considered the world's preeminent expert on ancient ship construction. I like to think of him as the 'wood whisperer.' As I explained to the team, Dick could read the wood in a hull the way you or I read a newspaper.

Due to other commitments Dick had only a narrow window of opportunity during which he could participate in the excavation, and funding his trip on such short notice initially proved problematic. The United States Ambassador to Israel at that time, Thomas E. Pickering, had a deep interest in archaeology and after I contacted the embassy the United States Information Service had arranged Dick's flight within 14 hours (!) of receiving the request.

Meanwhile, back at the lake…

Swollen from recent rains, the Sea of Galilee had started to advance towards the boat. When I had first seen the site, the lake had been about 30 meters (98 feet) away from the shoreline, but on the eve of the excavation the waters had approached to within 10 meters (33 feet) of the boat and the weather forecast called for yet more rain. If correct, the site would soon be inundated. We considered various proposals, up to and including lowering the level of the lake by pumping water from it, but by the time the excavation began, late on the afternoon of Sunday, February 16th, 1986, this problem remained unresolved.

The Excavation

The excavation had three objectives: to expose the boat and its surrounding area, to study the boat in situ, and to remove the hull for conservation to the nearby Yigal Allon Museum, which was under construction at that time. If possible we hoped to remove the boat intact, but from the outset this scenario seemed unlikely.

As night fell on that first day, I decided that we would work around the clock in a race against the rising lake waters. Gas fishing lamps lent an eerie atmosphere as the outline of the boat began to emerge.

During that evening, I received a visit from members of the Kinneret Authority, the Israeli governmental body responsible for

(above) The first night of excavation. The boat's stern is visible in the foreground.

(left) A frame, excavated during the first night of the excavation, indicated the excellent extent of the hull's survival in the sediment. (Photos: D. Syon. Courtesy Yigal Allon Museum.)

While enlarging the pit around the boat we were careful to leave a mud 'podium' to support the hull. (Photo: D. Syon. Courtesy Yigal Allon Museum.)

the lake. Once appraised of our situation, they proposed to protect the excavation site from the rising waters by constructing a massive earthwork and sandbag dike, and promised to return the next morning with equipment, materials and workers.

By 6 a.m. on the morning of February 17th, the lake's waters, whipped up by a strong *Sharkia* (easterly wind) had advanced so that they almost touched the site. The Kinneret Authority crew, with their heavy equipment and materials, arrived just in time and began to build a dike. Although the lake continued to rise, this issue ceased to be a problem for us, and indeed, the rising waters proved providential later in the process. We continued to remove the mud around the boat, forming a pit, while leaving a central mud 'podium' to support the hull. A pump worked around the clock removing the ground water that collected in the excavation pit.

The excavation had an amazing effect on everyone involved. Kibbutz Ginosar quite literally 'adopted' the excavation: its members were crucial to the project's success. They would finish their own work and then join us in the mud for stretches of eight and ten hours a day. People worked until they dropped. People from the neighboring modern settlement of Migdal, as well as from all over Israel, showed up and volunteered to help. Despite the tremendous pressures on all of us, we worked together as a team for a common purpose.

As the hull appeared from the mud, I asked Danny Syon, the team photographer, to pin white plastic string to the hull to indicate the planking seams, which were not always easy to identify because of cracks in the wood. Danny also tagged and numbered each timber. Removing the sediment from inside the boat was akin to

As we revealed the hull much effort went into ensuring that the timbers did not dry out. Here team members focus on a jury-rigged water sprinkler in the boat's bow. Note the white lines of plastic string that define planking seams and the red tags that were later numbered so that each timber received an independent identification number. (Photo: D. Syon. Courtesy Yigal Allon Museum.)

Detail of the bow, showing the unusual planking plan. Note the peculiar narrowness of some of the planks. *(Photo: D. Syon. Courtesy Yigal Allon Museum.)*

By the time hull-construction expert Dick Steffy (center in yellow shirt) arrived at the site, much of the hull had been cleared of sediment. *(Photo: D. Syon. Courtesy Israel Antiquities Authority.)*

Removing mud from the boat revealed the fragile wood. The team erected two iron bridges over the boat and covered them with a tarpaulin to shield the boat from the harsh sunlight. *(Photo: D. Syon. Courtesy Israel Antiquities Authority.)*

The stern's starboard section curved up and over the hull. Orna Cohen, the project conservator, tried to stabilize the stern with a polyurethane fill, but to no avail. That night the section collapsed. It was a sobering moment for all of us. *(Photo: D. Syon. Courtesy Yigal Allon Museum.)*

From the bridges the team lowered a hanging scaffold on which workers could lie for hours, carefully removing the mud by hand from inside the hull while avoiding damage to it. *(Photo: D. Syon. Courtesy Yigal Allon Museum.)*

sitting on a tree branch while cutting it off from the trunk: once we had removed the mud overburden inside the boat, we could no longer step there, as the waterlogged wood had a structural strength not unlike that of wet floral foam. To continue working inside the boat without touching it, kibbutz members constructed hanging scaffolding that allowed volunteers to continue work inside the boat without actually touching it. This framework did double duty, also supporting a tarpaulin that protected the wood from direct sunlight. By the time Dick arrived, much of the vessel's interior had been revealed.

While enlarging the pit around the boat we found remains of two more boats. These were examined summarily and recorded. We removed the uppermost timbers and buried the rest. To do otherwise would have required more resources than we could afford and could have endangered the main objective of saving the boat.

We completed the archaeological part of the excavation by our eighth day in the field. The remaining days focused on the conservation and the packaging of the boat for its removal to the Yigal Allon Museum, a distance of about 500 meters (1640 feet).

The surviving hull measures 8.2 meters (27 feet) in length by 2.3 meters (7.5 feet) in breadth and 1.2 meters (3.9 feet) in depth. The boat's timbers were waterlogged and could not support their own weight. Furthermore, the iron nails used to attach the frames to the hull were in excellent condition, precluding the possibility of disassembling the boat for removal. After consultations with

As the backhoe enlarged the pit surrounding the boat, we carefully monitored its activities. At the northwest side of the pit, we began to find loose pieces of ancient timbers. Zvika Malach, a volunteer from Moshav Migdal (center, with beard) noticed some timbers that seemed to be part of a solid structure. (Photo: D. Syon. Courtesy Israel Antiquities Authority.)

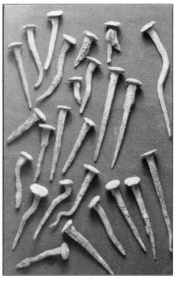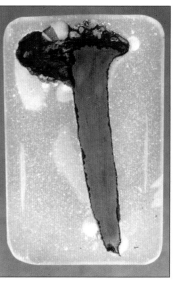

(above, left) Iron nails from the Galilee Boat. While the hull's planks were attached to each other with pegged mortise-and-tenon joints, the frames were attached to the planking with iron nails. (Courtesy Israel Antiquities Authority.)

(above, right) When Orna had one of the iron nails sectioned in a laboratory it was revealed to have less then a millimeter of rust, a result of having been protected by the anaerobic sediment in a freshwater environment. On shipwrecks found in the saline Mediterranean Sea, usually nothing remains of iron nails used in ancient hulls that have survived. (Courtesy Israel Antiquities Authority.)

Once the visible boat fragments were removed, we covered their find site (arrow) with sand bags and stopped enlarging that side of the pit. (Photo: D. Syon. Courtesy Yigal Allon Museum.)

numerous experts Orna Cohen, the project conservator, initiated a novel and innovative method for packaging the boat for transport. She decided to strengthen the hull internally and externally with fiberglass frames and trusses while covering the entire boat in a polyurethane 'straightjacket.'

Members of Ginosar, well versed in constructing and repairing the kibbutz's many boats, fashioned a fiberglass frame between each two original framing stations. Once they completed framing

the hull's interior, it was then covered with light plastic sheeting and spray filled with polyurethane, a process that took place at night under the light of the fishing lanterns. A company we had hired sprayed on the polyurethane as two dark liquids, which reacted when they came in contact, quickly turning into hard foam: under the gas lamplight, this process made it seem like a living organism engulfing the boat.

The following day we removed the awning and metal superstructure and then began excavating a series of tunnels into the mud 'podium' under the hull and perpendicular to it. In the process we came across additional elements of the vessel's construction. This process also revealed that the boat was sitting on a cradle. As workers completed each tunnel the team passed a fiberglass truss through and secured it around the hull's exterior. Then the tunnel itself was spray-filled with polyurethane, which quickly hardened into external supportive frames. Once the hull rested on a set of these, we removed the mud remaining between the polyurethane supports and repeated the process until the entire boat was protected in a synthetic 'cocoon.'

(left) Team members from Kibbutz Ginosar create internal fiberglass frames between the original framing stations. (Photo: D. Syon. Courtesy Israel Antiquities Authority.)

(right) Spraying on the polyurethane. (Photo: D. Syon. Courtesy Israel Antiquities Authority.)

Once the hull had been filled with polyurethane, the team removed the surrounding iron superstructure and began excavating a series of tunnels beneath the hull perpendicular to the keel. *(Photo: D. Syon. Courtesy Israel Antiquities Authority.)*

Work on the tunnels continued late into the night. Once the first series of tunnels were excavated, fiberglass trusses inserted and spray-filled, it was possible to repeat the procedure. *(Photo: D. Syon. Courtesy Yigal Allon Museum.)*

By the end of the process the entire boat had been entirely encased in a protective cocoon. *(Photo: D. Syon. Courtesy Israel Antiquities Authority.)*

We now reversed the pump that had been removing ground water from the excavation pit and began pumping lake water into the pit to raise the boat to the level of the lake. *(Photo: D. Syon. Courtesy Israel Antiquities Authority.)*

We then walked the boat out of the excavation pit… *(Photo: D. Syon. Courtesy Yigal Allon Museum.)*

…only to get stuck on a sand bank. We gently slid the boat over this… *(Photo: D. Syon. Courtesy Israel Antiquities Authority.)*

On February 26th, only eleven days and nights since the start of the excavation, we reversed the pump that had been preventing ground water from inundating the site, and began raising the water level in the excavation pit to approximate that of the lake. Concurrently, a steam shovel excavated a channel through the dike. Once it had been breached, we floated the boat, safe in her wrapping, out of the pit and for the first time in some two millennia she sailed the Sea of Galilee. The boat spent the night in Kibbutz Ginosar's small fishing harbor. The next day a large crane placed her on land, adjacent to where the outline of her conservation pool had been marked out on the ground. Within ten days, the Yigal Allon Museum built a reinforced concrete conservation pool. A crane then lifted the boat and placed her inside the pool.

The excavation, packaging and extraction of the boat had been a group effort: I could not have asked for better staff and volunteers.

…and the boat sailed out on the waters of the Sea of Galilee. The entire excavation had taken only eleven days and nights. For me it had seemed like years. (Photo: D. Syon. Courtesy Yigal Allon Museum.)

The next morning a small launch towed the boat to the Yigal Allon Museum. (Photo: D. Syon. Courtesy Yigal Allon Museum.)

(above, left) We floated the boat over a purpose-built frame and made final adjustments to make sure she was secure. (center) A crane then lifted the boat ashore next to the site selected for her conservation pool, seen here marked out in white chalk. (right) As the crane moved the boat, on its frame over the pool, the crane slipped off one of its improperly-placed moorings and, for a moment the boat hung precariously over the pool. I had the crane operator return the boat to its original position. The next day, with a different crane—and a different crane operator—the boat was safely placed in the pool. (Photos: D. Syon. Courtesy Israel Antiquities Authority and Yigal Allon Museum.)

Everyone involved in the project felt that they had a truly unique experience. One could not have asked for a more dedicated crew. (Courtesy Israel Antiquities Authority.)

THE CONSERVATION PROCESS

Stabilizing the boat was a long and arduous process directed by the team conservator, Orna Cohen. First it was necessary to remove the polyurethane jacket while at the same time constructing temporary supports for the boat. Once these tasks had been completed, the boat was submerged in water to prevent the wood from dehydrating until conservation could begin.

Subsequently, the Department of Antiquities built a metal structure with a viewers' gallery to protect the pool during the lengthy conservation process, while allowing viewing access to visitors. The revenue from the exhibition of the boat during this period helped fund her conservation.

The boat's survival over the millennia resulted from her being buried in the lake's soft silt, which protected her timbers from wood-eating organisms. This situation, however did not prevent the boat's timbers from becoming waterlogged. If left in an air environment without treatment the water inside the wood cells would evaporate causing the wood to shrink, fragment and crumble.

Orna selected a two-part process using polyethylene glycol

At this stage the Israel Department of Antiquities (the forerunner of today's Israel Antiquity Authority) had a metal structure built over the boat's conservation pool. It included a glass-partitioned visitors gallery, which allowed visitors to see the boat, or at least where she was being conserved, during the long conservation process. This helped fund the process. (Photo: D. Syon. Courtesy Israel Antiquities Authority.)

(PEG). This is a synthetic wax that is commonly used to stabilize waterlogged wood by allowing the wax to replace the water in the wood cells.

Once in the conservation pool, the boat was stabilized, sturdy fiberglass supports replaced the jury-rigged ones placed under the boat during removal of the polyurethane cocoon, and heating elements were attached to the sides of the pool. Ambassador Pickering graciously arranged for the donation of 40 tons of PEG from Jacobson Agencies, Ltd., a subsidiary of DOW Chemicals.

During this period of preparation, the pool's water became infested with tiny red wormlike mosquito larvae, which made work in the pool unpleasant. Orna considered adding an insecticide, but feared its possible harm to those working in the pool. Moshele Lufan came up with an elegant, and ecologically correct, solution to the problem. He stocked the pool with three large goldfish that went around merrily gobbling up the larvae. Within days the goldfish had cleared the water.

Removal of the polyurethane inside the cramped confines of the pool was exceptionally difficult and time consuming. Additionally, most of the volunteers had left, and we had to build supports for the boat as we removed the casing. We could not fill the pool with water until all the polyurethane had been removed, otherwise we would cause damage to the boat. It was a difficult and exhausting period, as can be seen in our faces. (Photo: D. Syon. Courtesy Israel Antiquities Authority.)

The conservation process took 11(!) years. It took three more years to design and build the exhibition hall and prepare the boat for its permanent home. On February 15th, 2000, after months of diligent preparation by Orna and her team, the boat was moved successfully to the specially-

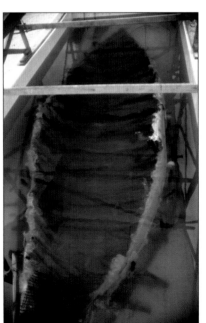

Orna oversees the removal of the polyurethane. (Photo: D. Syon. Courtesy Yigal Allon Museum.)

Finally. With all the polyurethane removed and the temporary supports in place we filled the pool with water. (Photo: D. Syon. Courtesy Israel Antiquities Authority.)

designed wing of the Yigal Allon Museum where she now rests. The exhibition opened to the public that year. Ever since then the Galilee Boat has become one of the most popular tourist destinations in Israel for Christian pilgrims and tourists alike.

The boat in the pool during the conservation process. Normally the boat was entirely immersed in her liquid bath. (Courtesy Yigal Allon Museum.)

At the completion of the conservation process, the PEG was drained from the pool and the boat was allowed to cool in a controlled manner. At this stage she looked like she had been dipped in candle wax. Orna and her team spent long hours carefully removing the excess wax using hair dryers and cotton cloth. (Courtesy Yigal Allon Museum.)

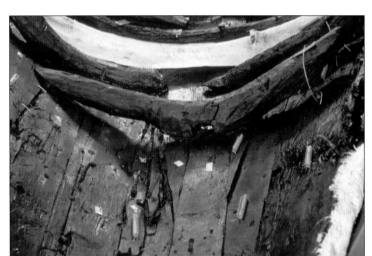

Detail of a section of the bow after it had been cleaned. (Courtesy Yigal Allon Museum.)

On February 15th, 2000, almost 14 years to the day to the beginning of the boat's excavation, Orna and her team moved the boat to the exhibition room in the Yigal Allon Museum in which she is now exhibited. (Courtesy Yigal Allon Museum.)

The boat during the set-up process. (Courtesy Yigal Allon Museum.)

The boat as she appears today, facing the port bow section. The upper edge of the far (starboard) side of the hull was the uppermost starboard strake that the Lufan brothers had originally noticed in the mud. (Photo: S. Wachsmann. Courtesy Institute of Nautical Archaeology.)

DISCUSSION

Dating the boat.—One of the most important aspects in understanding any ancient artifact is the ability to place it in its correct time frame. Three methods allowed us to date the boat: radiocarbon dating, hull construction techniques and ceramics.

Having an entire boat made out of wood allowed us to carry out radiocarbon dating on her. Ten samples taken from the boat's timbers provided an average date of 40 B.C., with a plus/minus factor of 80 years, thus framing the lifetime of the boat sometime between 120 B.C. and A.D. 40.

A comparative study of the ceramics found with the boat by David Adan-Bayawitz (Bar Ilan University) identifies the material as typical of the period from the latter part of the first-century B.C. to the decades following the mid-first century A.D., or until about the year A.D. 70. Production of these types of pottery ceases around the time of the First Jewish Revolt (A.D. 66–70). The absence of later pottery may be related to the destruction and depopulation of the nearby settlement of Migdal by the Roman army under the command of Vespasian in A.D. 67 (see below, pp. 31–32).

Dick Steffy independently came to more-or-less the same date range by comparing the construction techniques used in the boat to those prevalent on Mediterranean vessels.

"If this were a hull found in the Mediterranean," Dick wrote in his report to the Department, "I would date it between the first century B.C. and the second century A.D."

He emphasized, however, that construction traditions may have continued in the insular Sea of Galilee region long after they had gone out of use in the more cosmopolitan Mediterranean environment.

In truth, each of these three dating methods alone is insufficient, but taken together, they suggest a date for the boat between the first century B.C. and the first century A.D. Due to the use of recycled wood in the hull, discussed below, a later date within this framework is more probable.

Wood identification.—Ella Werker (Hebrew University, Jerusalem) studied samples from all of the boat's timbers to identify the different types of wood used in her construction and repairs. Ella's examination revealed that while most of the boat was constructed of cedar (*Cedrus*) planking and oak (*Quercus*) frames, the hull contained ten other wood genera: Aleppo pine (*Pinus halepensis*), Atlantic terebinth (*Pistacia atlantica*), carob (*Ceratonia siliqua*), hawthorn (*Crataegus*), laurel (*Laurus*), plane (*Platanus*), redbud (*Cercis siliquastrum*), sidder/Christ-thorn (*Ziziphus spina-christi*), sycamore (*Ficus sycomorus*) and willow (*Salix*). Examples of these trees are planted on the north side of the boulevard leading to the Yigal Allon Museum. All these genera are indigenous to the region except for cedar, which came from Lebanon.

Construction.—Dick Steffy concluded that the boat's builder was a master craftsman who probably learned his craft on the Mediterranean or, alternately, perhaps had been apprenticed to someone with that background. The timber used by the builder was far inferior to that utilized on contemporaneous Mediterranean

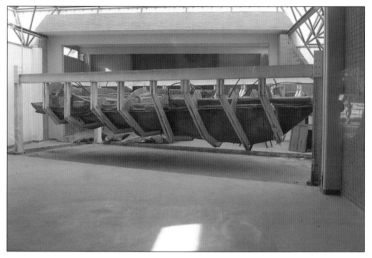

A boat of approximately the same age as the Galilee Boat was found at Herculanium in Italy. The vessel had been carbonized by a pyroclastic flow from the same volcanic eruption that buried the Roman city of Pompeii in A.D. 79. The builders of the Herculanium Boat, from near the epicenter of the Roman Empire, used first-rate timber in her construction. As opposed to this, the timber used in the Galilee Boat was largely of recycled and poor-quality wood. (Photo: S. Wachsmann)

The boat is a symphony of wood recycling. She is constructed largely of wood in secondary use and at the end of her work life, all reusable timbers were removed. Here, part of the boat's keel extending below the hull bears mortise scars, indicating that this timber had seen previous use. (Photo: D. Syon. Courtesy Israel Antiquities Authority.)

Nails and a dark stain indicate where a frame had been removed in antiquity, apparently for secondary use. (Photo: D. Syon. Courtesy Israel Antiquities Authority.)

The stern post was missing. I had assumed it had rotted away, but in fact it had been carefully removed from the hull in antiquity, for secondary use, severing the after keel scarf. (Photo: D. Syon. Courtesy Israel Antiquities Authority.)

vessels. Perhaps better materials were beyond the boat owner's financial ability. Many of the boat's timbers, including part of the keel, show signs of previous use on earlier vessels.

The boat had been repaired repeatedly during its long life, eventually ending on the scrap heap. Her reusable timbers, including frames, the stempost assembly and the sternpost, had been removed in antiquity.

Dick's careful examination of the hull revealed that the boat had carried a mast. Normally a mast is fitted into a mast step, which, depending on the vessel, may be a simple block of wood or a complicated construction. While we did not uncover a mast step in the boat, Dick found four nail holes and an impression of a now-missing mast step amidships atop the keel. This timber, like so many other reusable timbers of the boat, had been removed in antiquity for reuse. Thus, the boat could move under both sail and/or oars.

The remaining hull, old and useless, had been pushed out into the lake, perhaps with the intention of utilizing it as a future source for additional spare parts. The lake's sediments eventually buried it, however, and the old boat was forgotten.

Crews & passenger capacity.—One of my most memorable moments during the excavation took place during Dick's first day at the site. After he had studied the boat's construction for some time, he came over and showed me a rough outline of the vessel's profile plan (side view) as he understood it. In Dick's view the boat would have originally had a pointed prow and a high, recurving stern. I asked him how many rowers, in his opinion, it would have taken to row a vessel this size. Probably four, he told me.

No sooner had Dick returned to his recording than I received a visit by Fathers Stanislau Loffreda and Vigilio Corbo, two Franciscan priests who excavated at Capernaum and at Migdal. As I showed them around the excavation, they told me about a first-century A.D. mosaic depicting a boat, or a model of a boat, which they had uncovered a decade earlier at Migdal. Corbo drew a picture of the mosaic in my notebook. The vessel had a pointed bow and a recurving stern: it looked exactly like Dick's drawing. When later that day I showed Corbo's sketch to Dick, he remained convinced

that I was pulling a practical joke on him as the two images looked so alike.

The vessel depicted on the mosaic from Migdal showed what appeared to be three oars on its port side: this suggested that it had been rowed by a six-man crew, and based on Dick's assessment of a four-man rowing crew, my initial conclusion was that the vessel in the Migdal Mosaic represented a boat larger than the one that we were uncovering.

Much later, long after the excavation had been completed, I studied the mosaic in greater detail and realized that the two forward oars appeared as single lines of tesserae (mosaic stones) but that the sternmost oar widened at the bottom: in other words, what I had taken to be a 'third oar' was not an oar but rather a quarter rudder, used to steer the boat. This meant that the boat in the mosaic must have had four rowers, as Dick had suggested for our boat, and a helmsman: a minimum crew of five.

Both Josephus and the Gospel writers support the evidence of the Galilee Boat and the boat mosaic from Migdal regarding crew sizes. Josephus, who served as magistrate of the Galilee, describes how, during the Jewish Revolt (A.D. 66–70), he prepared at Migdal a sham 'war fleet' of boats that he brought against Tiberias to prevent its inhabitants from going over to the Roman side. Lacking an army, Josephus placed skeleton crews in each of the boats. He writes:

> Then he [Josephus] collected all the boats that he could find on the lake—some two hundred and thirty, with no more than four sailors in each—and with this fleet made full speed for Tiberias.
>
> The Jewish War II:635

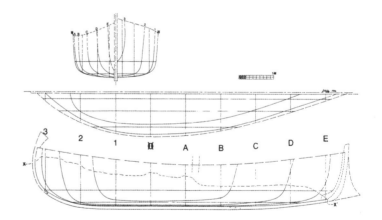

(above) Dick's lines drawings of the boat (facing right) and (below) the Migdal Boat Mosaic (facing left). (Photos: D. Syon. Courtesy Israel Antiquities Authority.)

Josephus, however, also makes repeated references to a captain or a helmsman in each of the boats when describing the taking of hostages from among the men of Tiberias:

I then summoned the heads of families and ordered each of them to launch a vessel, bring the steersman with them, and follow me to Tiberias.

Life of Josephus XXII:163

And:

As the boats were successively filled, he ordered the captains to make with all speed to Tarichaea [the Greek name of Migdal, literally 'salted fish'] and to lock the men in prison.

The Jewish War II:641

From Josephus' statements, above, we may reasonably create the following equation:

4 sailors + 1 helmsman/captain = 5 man crew

Now, the Gospels mention two specific boats, those of Zebedee and Simon Peter:

As he [Jesus] went a little farther, he saw James son of Zebedee and his brother John, who were in their boat mending the nets. Immediately he called them; and they left their father Zebedee in the boat with the hired men, and followed him.

Mark 1:19–20

Thus, Zebedee's boat had a crew of five or more men:

1 (Zebedee) + 1 (James) + 1 (John) + (2 + ?) ('hired servants') = 5 + ? man crew

Similarly, when Simon Peter decided to fish one evening, presumably in his own boat, six other Disciples worked with him, thus forming a seven-man crew:

Gathered there together were Simon Peter, Thomas called the Twin, Nathanael of Cana in Galilee, the sons of Zebedee and two others of his disciples. Simon Peter said to them, "I am going fishing." They said to him, "We will go with you." They went out and got into the boat, but that night they caught nothing.

John 21:2–3

This description can also be stated as an equation regarding the number of men crewing the boat that night:

1 (Simon Peter) + 1 (Thomas called the Twin) + 1 (Nathanael) + 2 (sons of Zebedee) + 2 ('other disciples') = 7-man crew

Again…a crew of five or more. As the boat presumably needed more hands than just the four rowers and helmsman in order to ply the nets when fishing, the two additional men do not change the basic conclusion that Simon Peter had the same type of boat. In other words, the Migdal Boat Mosaic, the writings of Josephus and the Gospels all seem to be describing the same type of watercraft, which is exemplified by the Galilee Boat.

How many men could a boat of this size carry? This was a question repeatedly asked of us during the excavation. Could the boat have carried 13 men—Jesus and his 12 Apostles? This image is indelibly linked to Jesus' ministry on the lake and, as we have seen, became a popular motif in Christian art as a result of the many nautical references in the Gospels to Galilean seafaring (Matthew 8:18,

23–27, 9:1, 14:13–14, 22–32, 15:39, 16:5; Mark 1:19–20, 4:35–41, 5:18, 21, 6:32–34, 45–51, 8:10, 13–14; Luke 5:1–11, 8:22–25, 37, 40; John 6:16–24).

It was only natural, therefore, that when I began collecting literary evidence pertaining to our boat that I read the Gospels carefully, and repeatedly, looking for instances that record Jesus sailing with the Twelve Apostles in a single boat. I was surprised when I finally realized that nowhere do the Gospels state that the Twelve accompanied Jesus on any recorded boat trip. Rather, the Gospels describe Jesus accompanied by his Disciples on these trips: the Book of Acts (1:15) records that Jesus had numerous disciples, thus, we cannot today determine how many people participated in any of the trips recorded in the Gospels.

Fortunately, Josephus supplies us with several references that do suggest the maximum capacity of these vessels. In describing his sham fleet against the city of Tiberias, he lists the men in his own boat:

I myself, with my friends and the seven soldiers already mentioned, then embarked and set sail for the city.

Life of Josephus XXXII:164

As the boat must also have had a crew, we can deduce that Josephus' boat held at least 15 men:

1 (Josephus) + 7 ("armed men") + (2 + ?) ("friends") + 4 (sailors) + 1 (helmsman/captain) = (15 + ?) men

During the action, Josephus twice describes captives taken on board his boats. This is how he describes the first vessel to take hostages on board:

Ten citizens, the principal men of Tiberias, came down; these he took on board one of the vessels and carried out to sea.

The Jewish War II:639

Here, also, the description allows us to conclude that the boat carried 15 men:

10 ("principal men of Tiberias") + 4 (sailors) + 1 (helmsman/captain) = 15 men

Although Josephus normally uses the Greek term *ploion* for "boat," in this case he specifically describes the vessel as "one of the fishing boats" (Greek: *mia ton haliathon*), indicating the primary function of these vessels.

Josephus provides us with one more clue regarding the carrying capacity of these boats. He records that he lured a total of 2,600 of Tiberias's leading citizens into the boats of his sham fleet to be held hostage in Migdal as security for the city's loyalty to the rebel cause. As we have seen, elsewhere he refers to collecting 230 boats to take part in this action. Although both numbers may be exaggerated, nevertheless the number of men per boat in this case remains remarkably similar to the previous calculations:

2,600 hostages ÷ 230 boats = 11–12 men per boat
11–12 hostages + 5-man crew = 16–17 men per boat

So, in summary, had Jesus wished to sail with the Twelve, then a vessel like the Galilee Boat could have easily carried all of them based on the evidence supplied to us by Josephus.

How much would 15 men have weighed? The load can be calculated based on the average height (1.66 meters, or 5 feet 5½

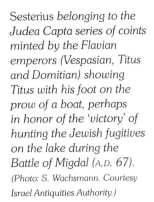

During the excavation, because we often continued excavating into the night and the mud inside came out in clumps, I had the team register all the mud from the boat and in a one-meter radius surrounding the boat as 'artifacts.' The mud was collected in plastic boxes and dumped in piles in a nearby field. Each pile had its own registration number. Following the completion of the excavation, team members examined the mud piles for artifacts. The most interesting artifact found in this process was a pyramidal iron arrowhead. (Photo: D. Syon. Courtesy Israel Antiquities Authority.)

inches) of skeletons of Roman-Byzantine period Galilean males. Current data on height/weight ratios indicate that they probably would have weighed about 62–63 kilograms (137–139 pounds) each. Thus, 15 men would have weighed about a ton and could have been transported in a vessel like the Galilee boat, although admittedly it might have been a tight fit.

Galilean Seafaring during the Roman and Byzantine periods.— During the Jewish Revolt (A.D. 66–70) the Sea of Galilee served as the base of operations for a fleet of boats based at Migdal, that employed the Jewish rebels against the Romans.

Josephus, who is our only source of information, was also a key actor in this drama, having served as the leader of the rebel forces in the Galilee until he defected to the Roman side. During one battle Josephus used boats to transport his men. When Josephus was wounded his army lacked leadership. Although Josephus' opponent could have won the battle, he instead retreated after receiving reports that reinforcements had sailed from Migdal. Josephus also relates how he escaped twice from angry mobs in Tiberias by commandeering a boat and sailing to Migdal.

Of the three nautical battles between Jews and Romans recorded by Josephus, the Battle of Migdal (A.D. 67) receives the most detailed description, perhaps because Josephus had witnessed it. When the Roman legions advanced on Tiberias, the city opened its gates to them and, thus, was spared destruction. The rebel forces in Tiberias abandoned it for Migdal, which had been previously fortified by Josephus and also had a large fleet at hand.

A rebel leader named Jesus Ben Sapphia led a boat-based commando raid against the Roman camp in which the Jews succeeded at pulling down part of the defensive wall before retreating to their vessels. Remaining within bowshot range the Jews engaged the pursuing Romans from their boats.

Later, when Migdal fell, the Jews took to their boats seeking refuge on the lake. Josephus relates that they could not escape to land because "all were in arms against them." The next day, the Roman general—soon to be emperor—Vespasian ordered the construction of 'rafts.' These were soon ready thanks to an abundance of timber and carpenters. Archers and infantry manned these vessels and attacked the fleeing Jews who were seeking safety on the lake.

This was not so much a battle as a slaughter. The Jews were no match for the Romans: the Jewish boats were smaller and their crews were greatly outnumbered. The boats that remained were driven ashore where the final phase of the 'battle' took place. Here many Jews were killed in the water as they tried to escape to shore, while others reached the beach only to be murdered by the Romans. Josephus describes the end of the conflict thus, "the beaches were

(above) The pyramidal iron arrowhead is of a type found at Gamla, in the Golan Heights (right), a site conquered by the Roman army under Vespasian immediately after the Battle of Migdal. This makes it likely that the arrowhead had been loosed during that conflict. It does not indicate, however, that this specific boat participated in the battle as the arrow to which it was affixed could have reached the boat's site subsequent to its abandonment. (Photo above: Courtesy Yigal Allon Museum. Photo right: S. Wachsmann.)

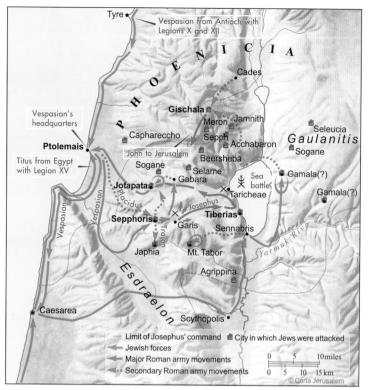

Vespasian's campaign in Galilee, A.D. 67.

strewn with wrecks. The dead, including those who earlier fell in the defense of the town, numbered six thousand seven hundred" (*The Jewish War* III:530–531).

Josephus employs the Greek word *sxedia* to describe the watercraft built by Vespasian for the Battle of Migdal. This term is usually translated as 'rafts', but the same term is also used by Homer to describe the vessel that Odysseus built to leave the island of Calypso (*The Odyssey* 5:251).

We may glean the following information about these vessels from Josephus' narrative:

- They were constructed quickly of wood by carpenters;
- They were bigger and could carry more men than the boats used by the fleeing Jews;
- They also appear to have been higher in the water than the boats used by the Jews, as the Roman soldiers were able to leap into the Jewish boats from the *sxedia*.
- Rafts are usually clumsy and slow, but Josephus relates that Vespasian's vessels overwhelmed the fast and maneuverable Jewish boats. This suggests that the *sxedia* were not simply 'Tom Sawyer'-type log rafts.

What, then, were these *sxedia*? Josephus may be describing catamarans that Vespasian's carpenters constructed quickly by fitting fighting platforms to pairs of the larger-class boats, like the Galilee Boat, left behind at Migdal by the Jews. The Romans were certainly familiar with catamaran construction, descriptions of which go back to the fifth-century B.C. Herodotus (IV: 88, 97) uses the term *sxedia* to describe the bridge built over the Bosporus by Darius, which consisted of a platform supported by boats and Alexander the Great lashed war galleys together to support siege machines during his conquest of Tyre (Diodorus Siculus XVII:46:1).

The Talmud contains numerous references to nautical subjects, including some describing boat traffic on the Sea of Galilee. In one case we read of "Kurdekaya that were brought up and sold from Susita to Tiberias" (PT *Shvi'it* 8:38a). This is apparently a reference to the transport by boat of a particular type of grain.

The Midrash used the swift boat crossing from the west bank of the lake to its east bank—"as from Tiberias to Susita"—as a metaphor for speed. This expression implies a regular commercial boat route existing between the two cities. This crossing had the predominant west wind at its back: the return crossing would have been made against the wind and, therefore, be much slower. Noah's ark is described in one source as sailing "on two *korot* as from Tiberias to Susita" (*Genesis Rabbah* 32:9; see also 31:13): that is, despite its burden the ark did not sit deep in the water, but rather sailed quickly.

Boats remained a common sight on the Sea of Galilee well into Islamic times. Mukaddasi noted in 985 that "around its shores are villages and palm trees, and on its surface are boats which come and go"; Idrisi in 1154 relates that over the lake "sail vessels that carry crops of the land around the lake to the city [Tiberias]."

Excessive taxation during the Ottoman period (1517–1920) reduced the number of boats on the Sea of Galilee drastically, a fact noted by both MacGregor and Twain. Following repeal of the tax during the British Mandatory period the number of boats increased. Today the lake is alive with boats and ships used chiefly for fishing, tourism and recreation.

Taken together, the textual evidence indicates that heavy water traffic existed on the Sea of Galilee during the Roman and Byzantine periods. This conclusion is supported by the many harbors built for this purpose around the lake at that time.

First-century A.D. *Galilean boats.*—In *The Jewish War* (III:523) Josephus describes the boats used by the Jews in the Battle of Migdal as "small and built for piracy" and emphasizes this as one of the reasons why the Jews were unsuccessful in the conflict against the Romans. He does not write that these boats were used for piracy, only that they were *built* for piracy. Indeed, it would be difficult to imagine a purpose for pirate boats on the Sea of Galilee as the lake is too small for brigands to remain undetected.

Josephus is presumably referring to characteristics that this Galilean type of boat had in common with the small craft used for piracy in the Mediterranean Sea, which was often conducted near shore. On such craft a shallow draft represented a distinct advantage as it allowed them to escape pursuit by larger craft and to be beached with relative ease. The Galilee Boat has a relatively flat bottom and vertical sides, with a tight turn of the bilge resulting in a minimal draft, which coincides with Josephus' description.

Based on a study of the Gospels, Josephus and contemporaneous imagery, it appears that at least two types of boats saw use on the Sea of Galilee during the first-century A.D. Alongside vessels like the Galilee Boat, a small type of boat probably existed on the lake, although the evidence for it remains meager. Still, it would be surprising if smaller vessels were not also in use.

The possible existence of a smaller boat type on the lake in the first century A.D. can be inferred from a story that Josephus relates. In it he and two bodyguards escaped from an angry crowd in Tiberias by jumping into a boat moored nearby and making a dash for Migdal (*The Jewish War* II:619; *Life of Josephus* XVIII:96).

The hasty getaway suggests that Josephus and his companions may have made use of a small rowboat.

In the Gospels, occasionally the diminutive for boat (Greek: *ploiarion*) is used in place of the standard term *ploion* (Luke 5:2–3; John 6:22–24, 21:3–8), but Anson Rainey has demonstrated that both terms refer to the same large type of boat (Wachsmann et al. 1990: 126).

The Jordan boat.—Jewish tradition refers to a 'Jordan Boat' (BT *Shabbat* 83b). In Orthodox Jewish interpretation ships and boats are generally considered ritually pure, but the Jordan Boat is not included in this general sanction because it was "loaded on dry land and lowered into the water." This vessel has been considered a small boat, used to transport cargoes on the Jordan, but this river never served as a commercially-viable water route. If navigation on the river was possible at all it could only have been in a southerly direction, making use of the current: returning north was impossible.

Given these considerations, the term 'Jordan Boat' is best understood as referring to ferry crossings over the Jordan River. This consisted of a boat or a floating platform that could be pulled across by a rope attached on the east and west banks of the river. We read of such ferry crossings over the Jordan in connection to the uprising of Absalom against David (2 Samuel 17:20, 22; 19:17–18): two such ferries appear in the sixth-century A.D. Madeba mosaic.

The 'Jordan Boat' mentioned in Jewish sources may refer to ferry crossings over the Jordan River. Two such ferries are depicted on the Byzantine-period Madeba Map. *(byzantio.tumblr.com)*

Boats on the Sea of Galilee during the Nineteenth and Twentieth Centuries.—Descriptions of the larger boats used on the Sea of Galilee prior to the introduction of motorized transport display remarkable similarities to the Galilee Boat. John MacGregor, who visited the lake in the mid-nineteenth century (see above, pp. 15–17), notes that the largest boats on the lake were about 30 feet (9.14 meters) long, with a breadth of 7 feet (2.13 meters). In comparison, the Galilee boat, with some of its parts removed in antiquity, is 8.2 meters (27 feet) long and 2.3 meters (7.5 feet) in breadth. Intuitively, MacGregor suggests that this was the larger limit of ancient craft plying the lake:

MacGregor's illustration of a fishing boat at Bethsaida. *(From MacGregor 1870: 371.)*

The boats now used on the lake by the fishers are about the same size, rowing five oars, but very clumsy ones, and with a very slow stroke. Generally only three oars were in use, and I much regret that I failed to remark whether there was a rudder, but I think there was none. Their build is not on bad lines and rather "ship-shape," with a flat floor, likely to be a good sea-boat, sharp and rising at both ends, somewhat resembling the Maltese. The timbers are close and short pieces, the planks "carvel built," and daubed with plenty of bitumen for that is readily obtainable here…. The waist is deep and there are no stern sheets, but a sort of stage aft.

John MacGregor, *The Rob Roy on the Jordan, Nile, Red Sea & Gennesareth, &c.*: 357–358

James Hornell, a British expert on indigenous craft, studied boats on the Sea of Galilee, during his visit to Mandatory Palestine. The largest vessel type recorded by Hornell on the lake, termed *Arabiye*, was 7.2 meters (23.6 feet) long with a beam of 2.4 meters (7.9 feet). Like the Galilee Boat, the *Arabiye* served primarily for fishing with the seine net and had decks fore and aft.

Arabiye boats at Tiberias in the early twentieth century. *(From Nun 1989: 30.)*

Influence of the seine net on Sea of Galilee boat construction.—The seine net was the largest and most valuable net used in fishing on the Sea of Galilee. In modern times, the net could be from 150 to 400 meters (492–1,312 feet) long and required ten to 20 fishermen to deploy it. The net had ropes about 70 meters (230 feet) long at either extremity and was 2 meters (6.6 feet) high at the sides, rising to 5–6 meters (16–20 feet) in the middle.

A seine net is used to surround and then to trap shoals of fish between it and the shore, hence Jesus' description (see above, pp. 8–9). Our English term 'seine' derives from the Greek term *segena*, which is the specific term used by Jesus in this parable. The same net is known as a *cherem* in Hebrew and a *jarf* in Arabic.

Fishing with a seine net as depicted in the Egyptian tomb painting of Puimre at Thebes (XVIIIth Dynasty, 15th century B.C.). (After N. d. G. Davies 1922. The Tomb of Puyemrê at Thebes I: The Hall of Memories. New York: Metropolitan Museum of Art: pl. XV.)

The boat is used for only part of the process when fishing with a seine net: after the shoal of fish is trapped the fishermen pull the catch to land. Thus, much of the effort in catching the fish with a seine net is expended on land while the boat spends much of this time beached or riding at anchor. The Talmud terms this "to stand the boat" (*leha'amid et hasfina*). On the Sea of Galilee, the fishermen of Tiberias were particularly known for their use of the seine net and are referred to as "the seiners of Tiberias" (*charmei Teveriah*).

Nun supplies a detailed description of the handling of a seine net, which was still used by fishermen on the Sea of Galilee until recent times. The net is carried on the vessel's stern deck. When everything is ready and a shoal of fish has been detected near shore, the boat moves to the starting point. Half of the crew remains on land holding the first rope, while the net is spread as the boat advances quietly under oar perpendicular to the shore. When all the rope at one end of the net have dropped into the lake, the boat turns, now advancing parallel to the coast, until all the net has slipped over the stern into the water. When this is completed, the boat returns to shore letting out the remaining ropes.

When the boat lands, the remaining crew members disembark and, taking the rope, begin to pull the net to shore as do their counterparts at the other end of the net, thus capturing the fish between the net and the shore, as illustrated in numerous Egyptian tomb paintings depicting everyday life.

The seine net appears to have had two basic influences on the large class of boats used on the Sea of Galilee:

• First, it defined the largest size of fishing boat required on the lake as one capable of deploying a seine net. This size, about

7–9 meters (23–29.5 feet) long, holds true for both the two-millennium-old Galilee Boat and for the *Arabiye* boats recorded by Hornell and MacGregor on the Sea of Galilee. There is no reason to believe that this optimum size changed in the interim.

• Second, the seine net requires a large stern deck on which to load it. Hornell notes this structural detail in relation to the *Arabiye* boats. The Galilee Boat did not survive to deck height at stem or stern, however, Dick concluded that it must have originally supported a stern deck based on the surviving structure.

This latter consideration may clarify a passage in the New Testament. All three Synoptic Gospels refer to Jesus sleeping during a boat trip with his disciples. The Gospel of Mark, however, adds two interesting details:

> *A great windstorm arose, and the waves beat into the boat, so that the boat was already being swamped. But he was in the stern, asleep on the cushion; and they woke him up and said to him, "Teacher, do you not care that we are perishing?"*
>
> Mark 4:37–38

Why did Jesus choose to sleep at the stern? One possible explanation is the existence of the large stern deck for the seine net. Anyone sleeping upon the stern deck of a vessel similar to the Galilee Boat would have been at the mercy of the weather and in the way of the helmsman. On the other hand, the area beneath the stern deck would have afforded the best shelter in the entire boat.

And what of "the cushion"? Scholars have noted that the definite article used in relation to this item indicates that it must have been part of the boat's equipment. The most likely explanation for it is one I heard from a veteran Arab Christian fisherman from Jaffa, Mussa Shibli, who related to me one day how in his youth he had participated in fishing with a seine net on sailing boats on the Mediterranean Sea.

He explained that the boats would normally carry sandbags for ballast. The fishermen used two types of bags: one was a heavy bag, weighing 50–60 kilograms (110–132 pounds), which in Arabic was called a *kis zabura*, which means 'balance or ballast sack,' or alternately two smaller sand bags, each weighing about 25 kilograms (55 pounds) and called *mechadet zabura*, which in Arabic means 'balance or ballast cushion.' These sandbags served to trim the boat when under sail. When not in use they were stored under the stern deck where they could be used as cushions on which crewmen could rest.

The model.—A 1:10 scale model of a generic first-century A.D. Sea of Galilee fishing boat is on exhibit in the foyer of the Yigal Allon Museum, near the entrance to the Galilee boat's large exhibition hall. Started in 1990, the model was built by William 'Bill' H. Charlton, a graduate student at Texas A&M University and INA's Dive Safety Officer, under Dick Steffy's guidance. Bill made his scale drawings working with actual measurements and lines drawings, field sketches, photomosaics of the boat and the final excavation report, while also incorporating iconographic and ethnographic evidence.

Bill selected pear wood for the model due to its close grain and ability to withstand changes in humidity. As this

The 1:10 scale model of a generic first-century A.D. fishing boat exhibited with the Galilee Boat. *(Photos: J. Lyle. Courtesy the Institute of Nautical Archaeology.)*

The model at an early phase of its construction. Bill Charlton is seen here placing a garboard plank on the model. *(Photo: J. Lyle. Courtesy the Institute of Nautical Archaeology.)*

Attaching the frames to the model. *(Photo: J. Lyle. Courtesy the Institute of Nautical Archaeology.)*

The Galilee Boat and Bill's model appear on an Israeli stamp sheet on a background of the Sea of Galilee and the city walls of Tiberias. The stamp was issued for the 1999 World Stamp Expo in Australia. *(Photo: S. Wachsmann.)*

was intended as a display, rather than a research model, the planks were glued to one another instead of being attached with pegged mortise-and-tenon joinery as in the ancient boat.

The model includes a mast, as well as fore and aft decks. The sail is made of linen, a material found in the ancient world long before the introduction of cotton. The model's lines were hand made from leaf fibers of the Torry yucca plant. Rope makers in the Sea of Galilee region would have chosen a similar indigenous plant, perhaps a reed or grass.

Bill labored on the model for 18 months. Funding for this project came from the Meadows Professorship of Biblical Archaeology, Texas A&M University. In 1992 the model was donated for permanent exhibition with the Galilee Boat.

The boat in the pool after completion of the conservation process. (Courtesy Israel Antiquities Authority.)

CONCLUSIONS

This review indicates that virtually all of the historical and iconographical evidence relating to seafaring on the Sea of Galilee in the first century A.D. refers to a large type of boat typified by the Galilee Boat. These vessels normally had a crew of five, but could accommodate as many as fifteen men, inclusive of crew. Relatively expensive, boats of this size normally would have been owned and operated by a family. When additional hands were needed, they could be hired.

This type of vessel served primarily for fishing and had evolved specifically for use with the large and heavy seine nets. This consideration apparently defined the optimal size of these boats: they had to be of sufficient dimensions to deploy the net and carry the crew required to work the boat and net. The boats had large stern decks on which they carried the net and from which it could be spread. Judging from recent ethnological parallels on the Sea of Galilee, they also probably had a smaller deck at the bow, but were open amidships.

These boats also transported passengers and supplies across the lake. In times of war, the vessels could be pressed into service, mainly as rapid troop carriers. With their shallow draft, they would have been ideally suited for swift commando attacks on the shelving shores that predominate in the Sea of Galilee: in this characteristic they apparently were similar to contemperaneous small boats used in coastal piracy on the Mediterranean. Both the Galilee Boat and the Migdal boat mosaic suggest that vessels of this type had a cutwater at their bows and could move under both square sail and/or oars.

Finally, based on crew sizes, it is possible to prove beyond reasonable doubt that the Galilee Boat represents the type of boat described in the Gospels in relation to Jesus' ministry, as well as by Josephus in his descriptions of boats on the lake during the First Jewish Revolt against Rome. At present we have no proof that this particular ancient boat played any part in these momentous events, but it is a veritable porthole into the past, allowing us to better understand seafaring on the Sea of Galilee in the times of Jesus.

GLOSSARY

I have endeavored throughout this volume to avoid technical terms when possible. Some terminology is unavoidable, however, particularly when describing details of nautical construction. This glossary is aimed at clarifying these terms. The nautical terms are derived from Steffy 1994: 266–298 and F. Hocker, 1998, Glossary of Nautical Terms. In Wachsmann, S., *Seagoing Ships and Seamanship in the Bronze Age Levant*. College Station and London, Texas A&M University Press and Chatham Press. 1998: 377–381.

aft.—Towards the stern.

Akkadian.—A Semitic language written in a cuneiform script.

amidships.—In the middle of the vessel.

anchor.—A device used to hold a vessel to the sea floor by means of a hawser.

Aramaic.—The predominant Semitic language spoken by Jews in their homeland during the time of Jesus.

ballast.—Weighty material placed low in a vessel to improve its stability.

bilge.—The area of a hull's bottom on which it would rest if grounded.

bitumen.—A natural hydrocarbon substance, such as asphalt, used as pitch.

bow.—a) The forward part of a ship; b) a flexible weapon used to shoot an arrow.

brails.—Lines that control the area of sail exposed to the wind.

brailed rig.—A sail system that employs brails.

caprail.—Timber attached to the top of a vessel's frames, which is normally the upper edge of a vessel's sides.

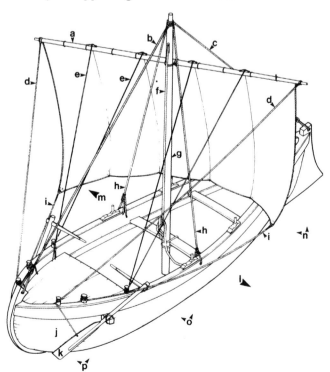

Rigging (brailed rig) and general terms relating to ships and boats: a) yard; b) backstay; c) forestay; d) braces; e) brails; f) halyard; g) mast; h) shrouds; i) sheets; j) quarter; k) quarter rudder; l) starboard (right); m) port (left); n) bow; o) amidships; p) stern. (Drawing: F. Hocker. Courtesy Institute of Nautical Archaeology.)

caulk.—To drive fibrous material into planking seams and to cover it with pitch to make a vessel's seams watertight.

catamaran.—A watercraft with twin parallel hulls.

cordage.—General term for ropes or cables.

cradle.—A structure for supporting a vessel out of water.

cuneiform.—Early form of wedge-shaped writing originating in Mesopotamia.

cutwater.—Forwardmost part of a vessel's stem that parts the water.

deck.—A horizontal platform placed across the interior of a vessel's hull.

draft.—The depth to which a hull is immersed in water.

edge joinery.—A form of hull construction prevalent in the Mediterranean region in antiquity, in which individual planks are joined to one another at their narrow edges.

floor (timber).—A frame timber that crosses the keel and spans the bottom of the hull.

forestay.—Line running from the masthead forward.

frame.—Transverse timber that supports or reinforces the hull planking.

futtock.—A framing member that extends the line of a floor timber or a half frame.

garboard strake.—The first strake on either side of the keel.

half frame.—A frame the heel or bottom of which begins near one side of the keel and spans part, or all, of one side of the hull. Half frames were normally used in pairs on either side of the keel.

halyard.—Lines employed in hoisting and lowering a sail.

hawser.—A heavy rope, normally used for mooring or towing.

Holy Temple.—The Babylonian king Nebuchadnezzar destroyed the first Holy Temple, built by Solomon in Jerusalem and exiled the Jews to Babylonia in 586 B.C. Upon their return to their homeland under Cyrus the Great, the Jews built the Second Holy Temple. This temple was enlarged repeatedly, notably by King Herod the Great (37–4 B.C.), before being destroyed by the Romans under Titus in A.D. 70.

hook scarf.—Attachment of two planks or timbers, and angular ends of which are offset to lock the joint. Hook scarfs are sometimes locked with wedges or keys.

hull.—The body of a watercraft.

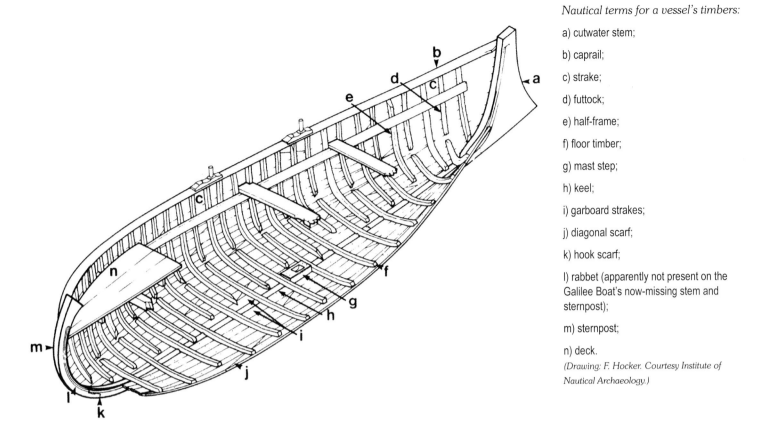

Nautical terms for a vessel's timbers:

a) cutwater stem;

b) caprail;

c) strake;

d) futtock;

e) half-frame;

f) floor timber;

g) mast step;

h) keel;

i) garboard strakes;

j) diagonal scarf;

k) hook scarf;

l) rabbet (apparently not present on the Galilee Boat's now-missing stem and sternpost);

m) sternpost;

n) deck.

(Drawing: F. Hocker. Courtesy Institute of Nautical Archaeology.)

in situ.—In its original location.

keel.—The main longitudinal timber in most hulls, which serves as a vessel's 'backbone.'

kosher.—Food that conforms to Jewish dietary laws.

lee.—The direction away from the wind.

lines.—General term for cordage or ropes on a watercraft.

lines drawings.—A set of geometric projections, usually arranged in three views, that illustrates the shape of a vessel's hull.

mast.—A spar used to support a sail and its associated rigging.

mast step.—Wooden block, or assembly of blocks, placed above the keel into which the mast is stepped, or secured.

mortise.—A cavity cut into a timber to receive a tenon.

mortise-and-tenon joinery.—A method for attaching planks or timbers to each other by means of projecting pieces (tenons) that are fitted into one or more cavities (mortises) of corresponding size.

pitch.—A dark, sticky substance used in caulking planking seams and waterproofing hulls.

port.—a) harbor; b) left side of a vessel.

quarter.—The after part of a vessel's sides.

quarter rudder.—Rudder affixed to the side of a hull at the stern.

rabbet.—Groove or cut made in a piece of timber so that the edges or another piece can be fitted into it to form a tight joint.

rigging.—General term for the lines (ropes) used in conjunction with masts, yards and sails.

sail.—a) A fabric used to drive a watercraft by wind power; b) the use of sail power to propel a vessel.

scarf.—An overlapping joint used to connect two planks or timbers without increasing their dimensions.

Sharkia (Hamsin).—Strong easterly wind in the region of Israel.

starboard.—Right side of a vessel.

stem.—The forwardmost timber, which is scarfed into the keel.

stern.—The after end of a vessel.

sternpost.—Vertical or upward-curving timber attached to the stern end of the keel.

strake.—A continuous line of planks extending from bow to stern.

Talmud.—Collection of Jewish law and tradition, consisting of the Mishna and the Gemara.

tenon.—a) wooden projection cut from the end of a timber; b) a separate wooden piece shaped to fit into a corresponding mortise.

tessera (pl. tesserae).—A small stone or other material used in a mosaic.

timbers.—All wooden hull members.

turn of the bilge.—The portion of the lower hull where a vessel's bottom curves towards its sides.

Ugaritic.—A cuneiform alphabetic script that evolved in the city of Ugarit, in Syria, during the Late Bronze Age.

yard.—A spar employed to spread a sail.

BIBLIOGRAPHY

Charlton Jr., W. H.
1992   Building a Model of the Kinneret Boat. *INA Quarterly* 19(3): 3–6.
2005   Modeling the Fishing Boat from the Sea of Galilee, Israel. In *Beneath the Seven Seas: Adventures with the Institute of Nautical Archaeology*, edited by G. F. Bass. New York: Thames & Hudson: 89–91.

Cohen, O.
2005   Conservation of the Ancient Boat from the Sea of Galilee. *Atiqot* 50: 219–232.

Coogan, M. D.
1978   *Stories from Ancient Canaan*. Philadelphia: Westminster Press: 92.

Hornell, J.
1935   *Report on the Fisheries of Palestine.*

MacGregor, J.
1870   *The Rob Roy on the Jordan, Nile, Red Sea, and Gennesareth, &C.: A Canoe Cruise in Palestine and Egypt, and the Waters of Damascus*. New York: Harper & Bros, 1870.

Notley, R. S.
2014   Genesis Rabbah 98:17—"And Why Is It Called Gennosar?" Recent Discoveries at Magdala and Jewish Life on the Plain of Gennosar in the Early Roman Period. In *Talmuda de-Eretz Israel: Archaeology and the Rabbis in Late Antique Palestine*. S. Fine and A. Koller, eds. Boston & Berlin, De Gruyter: 141–157.

Nun, M.
1964   *Ancient Jewish Fishery*. Merhavia: Hakibbutz Hameuchad Publishing House, Ltd. (in Hebrew).
1989   *The Sea of Galilee and its Fishermen in the New Testament*. Ein Gev: Kibbutz Ein Gev Tourist Department and the Kinnereth Sailing Co.
1992   *Sea of Galilee: Newly Discovered Harbours From New Testament Days*. Ein Gev: Kibbutz Ein Gev Tourist Department and the Kinnereth Sailing Co. (Third Revised Edition).
1993   *Ancient Stone Anchors and Net Sinkers from the Sea of Galilee*. Ein Gev: Kibbutz Ein Gev Tourist Department and the Kinnereth Sailing Co.
1993   Cast Your Net Upon the Waters: Fish and Fishermen in Jesus Time. *Biblical Archaeology Review* 19(6): cover, 46–56, 70.
1996   *The Land of the Gadarenes: New Light on an Old Sea of Galilee Puzzle*. Kibbutz Ein Gev: Kibbutz Ein Gev Sea of Galilee Fishing Museum.
1999   Ports of Galilee: Modern Drought Reveals Harbors from Jesus' Time. *Biblical Archaeology Review* 25(4): cover, 18–31, 64.

Pococke, R.
1743   *A Description of the East, And Some Other Countries*. London: Printed for the author.

Reich, R.
1991   A Note on the Roman Mosaic at Magdala on the Sea of Galilee. *Liber Annuus* 41:455–458, pls. 53–54.

Steffy, J. R.
1987   The Kinneret Boat Project. II: Notes on the Construction of the Kinneret Boat. *International Journal of Nautical Archaeology* 16: 325–329.
1994   *Wooden Ship Building and the Interpretation of Shipwrecks*. College Station, Texas A&M Press: 65–67.

Twain, M.
1870   *The Innocents Abroad, or, The New Pilgrims' Progress: Being Some Account of the Steamship Quaker City's Pleasure Excursion to Europe and the Holy Land: with Descriptions of Countries, Nations, Incidents, and Adventures As They Appeared to the Author*. Hartford, Conn: American Publishing Company.

Vilnay, Z.
1978   *Legends of Galilee, Jordan and Sinai: The Sacred Land*. Vol. 3. Philadelphia: Jewish Publication Society of America.

Wachsmann, S.
1988   The Galilee Boat: 2,000-Year-Old Hull Recovered Intact. *Biblical Archaeology Review* 14(5): 18–33.
2009   *The Sea of Galilee Boat*. College Station, Texas A&M University Press (Third Edition).

Wachsmann, S. et al.
1990   *The Excavations of an Ancient Boat from the Sea of Galilee (Lake Kinneret)*. Atiqot 19. Jerusalem, Israel Antiquities Authority.

Werker, E.
2005   Identification of the Wood in the Ancient Boat from the Sea of Galilee. *Atiqot* 50: 233–236, plans 1–2.